T0013297

"In the Kingdom of God, ashes turn to victories. Yet the chal powerless lives because they don't realize the connection they have access to. In *Grace Ambassador*, John Jackson brings a message of hopeful expectation as he unveils the epidemic of a powerless gospel that has been preached from the pulpit and practiced in the pews of our churches for far too long. The world is in desperate need of the Body of Christ to move from observation to activation and for Jesus to receive His full reward. In this catalytic book lies an essential message for the Church today. I highly recommend this book to anyone who is eager to step into the fullness of their calling as a believer, bring heaven to earth and become a true grace ambassador."

Kris Vallotton, senior associate leader, Bethel Church, Redding, CA; co-founder, Bethel School of Supernatural Ministry; author, *The Supernatural Ways of Royalty*, *Spiritual Intelligence*, *Poverty, Riches & Wealth* and more

"In *Grace Ambassador*, my dear friend Dr. John Jackson opens his heart to the world. If you truly believe the words on the pages of the Bible, you have a responsibility to join Jesus in bringing heaven to earth. Dr. Jackson will guide you as you discover your God-given abilities and use them to usher the grace and love of Christ into the here and now."

Samuel Rodriguez, lead pastor, New Season Worship; president/CEO, National Hispanic Christian Leadership Conference; author, *Persevere with Power*; executive producer *Breakthrough* and *Flamin' Hot*

"It's easy to wonder why there's such a gap between ideas and the realities of the Church. John Jackson helps us see where we've strayed and provides powerful tools to get us back on track. This Spirit-filled and deeply vulnerable book is a gift to us all. Don't miss it!"

Margaret Feinberg, author, *More Power to You*

"Dr. John Jackson has done it again! He has a way of re-introducing you to ancient words so you experience them as if it were the first time. As you read *Grace Ambassador*, prepare to meet grace and experience the Kingdom in a fresh and new way. Thanks, John!"

Albert Tate, pastor, Fellowship Church, Monrovia, CA; author, *How We Love Matters*

"We are living in a chapter of history where so much is at stake. It will require nothing less than heaven-inspired strategies to answer the world's most pressing problems through a new generation of reformers. With his new book, my good friend Dr. John Jackson has released a timely call to action for believers everywhere. *Grace Ambassador* wisely instructs, encourages and equips. It is honest and heartfelt and clearly communicates what the Body of Christ needs to hear in this crucial season. This is the Church's finest hour, and God wants to use *you* to bring about transformation in your sphere of influence!"

Dr. Ché Ahn, president, Harvest International Ministry; senior pastor, Harvest Rock Church, Pasadena, CA; international chancellor, Wagner University

"Dr. John Jackson is the leading voice for Christians of impact ready to use their purpose. His insight and work continue to inspire and equip leaders of all ages to get involved in changing the culture."

Gabrielle Bosché, co-founder and CEO, The Purpose Company

GRACE
AMBASSADOR

GRACE
AMBASSADOR

BRINGING HEAVEN
TO EARTH

DR. JOHN JACKSON

Chosen

a division of Baker Publishing Group
Minneapolis, Minnesota

Published by Chosen Books
Minneapolis, Minnesota
www.chosenbooks.com

Chosen Books is a division of
Baker Publishing Group, Grand Rapids, Michigan

Printed in the United States of America

Library of Congress Cataloging-in-Publication Data
Names: Jackson, John, 1961– author.
Title: Grace ambassador : bringing heaven to earth / Dr. John Jackson.
Description: Minneapolis, Minnesota : Chosen Books, a division of Baker
    Publishing Group, [2023] | Includes bibliographical references.
Identifiers: LCCN 2022037939 | ISBN 9780800762834 (trade paper) | ISBN
    9780800763138 (casebound) | ISBN 9781493439348 (ebook)
Subjects: LCSH: Grace (Theology) | Christian life.
Classification: LCC BT761.3 .J33 2023 | DDC 234—dc23/eng/20220912
LC record available at https://lccn.loc.gov/2022037939

Baker Publishing Group publications use paper produced from sustainable forestry practices and post-consumer waste whenever possible.

23 24 25 26 27 28 29   7 6 5 4 3 2 1

Contents

Foreword

We live in an age of celebrity. Athletes, actors and social media influencers have become the rage in our day. Unfortunately, that has spread to the Church, with too many high-profile leaders and too little emphasis on the everyday believer who faithfully lives for Jesus. But when you read the New Testament, you get a different picture. Ordinary people like fishermen become disciples. So do formerly despised people like tax collectors. Add to that the many anonymous characters in the gospels (the woman at the well, the man born blind, the Gadarene demoniac and so many more), and you realize that God does the extraordinary through the ordinary. In Acts, we read of unnamed men who come to Antioch, reaching people and planting a church that would send out missionaries (see Acts 11:19–26).

The New Testament elevates the unlikely and celebrates the overlooked. Women are given status by the gospel writers far above the culture of the day. Marginalized people like the widows neglected of food in Acts 6 become a key focus of change in the early Church. Paul celebrates how God uses what the world calls foolish and weak for His purposes (see 1 Corinthians 1:27).

The Church has become introverted and isolated from the world Jesus calls us to impact. In Acts, every believer was involved in sharing Christ and every believer was empowered by the Spirit (see Acts 4:31). They shared with one another in need and worshiped together as one. In our divided and confused world, we need the Church to equip and release every believer to show and share Jesus.

In *Grace Ambassador* John Jackson calls the Church to do just that. He exhorts the Church to return to a biblical focus on every believer being an ambassador for Jesus regardless of vocation or location. He challenges the clergy-laity separation that has, unintentionally or not, put most of God's servants on the sidelines of ministry.

Jackson further puts his finger on another ongoing issue hindering the Church in her call to fulfill the Great Commission: the sacred-secular divide. A result of this thinking is what I call "clergification," where we draw a line between those in vocational ministry—like pastors and missionaries—and all other believers. Jackson calls believers to break out of such dichotomies and to be on mission daily. He shows how to be engaged in the culture, to represent Christ across vocations and to employ spiritual gifts in daily life.

This is not a passive book. It calls for something revolutionary, a second Reformation that will distribute grace through ambassadors for Christ across the globe. Only when every believer understands his or her calling to be salt and light in our world can we be all God called us to be; this book will help you to understand why and how to do this.

Ed Stetzer, Wheaton, Illinois

Acknowledgments

I want to acknowledge the greatest act in human history of bringing heaven to earth. I thank my Lord and Savior, Jesus Christ, for being willing to forgo His position in heaven and be born a Babe in the manger and grow up to be the Man on the cross, where He shed His blood for my sins. Laid in the tomb, He rose on the third day and commissioned His followers to bear witness and be heavenly ambassadors of grace across the history and geography of earth.

My wife, Pam, our children and their spouses and our grandchildren are the great joys of my life, and I thank them for their great grace in the midst of my shortcomings. I am grateful for the church communities in Buena Park, Oxnard, Carson Valley and across California, Nevada and the Mountain West, where I have been privileged most often to teach and lead. I have always been in need of great grace and am grateful for receiving it from so many throughout the years.

I want to extend my thanks to Kim Bangs and all the team members at Chosen/Baker for their support and expertise throughout this project.

Finally, a word of thanks to the board and community at William Jessup University, where I am pleased to serve as president. I am again in the debt of many for the privilege of joining with you, in partnership with the Church, to equip transformational leaders for the glory of God. I pray that a generation of grace ambassadors will be stirred up and will rise to meet the opportunities of this new season.

I believe that God wants to transform lives, homes, churches, communities and cultures through the power of the Holy Spirit to bring heaven to earth through grace distributed, in the strong name of Jesus.

1

HOW I BECAME
A GRACE AMBASSADOR

I have a confession to make. It is not one I make lightly. You see, I have been a Christian for virtually my entire life; I have read the Bible diligently, almost every day without fail; and I have been a pastor and spiritual leader for more than forty years. So my confession to you is difficult. But if I am to write this book authentically to you the reader, I have to start with it.

Here is my confession: *I have often read the Bible and not believed the words on the page.*

Whew. Those were hard words to write. I hope you will keep reading and not stop. I am simply trying to be honest. There are hundreds of examples of how this has been true in my life (and maybe in yours as well). But for the purposes of this book, I want to center on one particular example. It is from a familiar part of the Bible, commonly called the Lord's Prayer:

"This, then, is how you should pray: 'Our Father in heaven, hallowed be your name, your kingdom come, your will be done, on earth as it is in heaven. Give us today our daily bread. And forgive us our debts, as we also have forgiven our debtors. And lead us not into temptation, but deliver us from the evil one.'"

Matthew 6:9–13

I believe and have always believed every word in that prayer that Jesus taught His disciples. **Except for the phrase I did not really believe.** It is a struggle, even now, to write this. But it is the truth. What are the words I did not believe? *Your will be done, on earth as it is in heaven.*

Honestly, I thought those words were the spiritual equivalent of a Hallmark card—you know, a great sentiment that was never going to be reality but represented the best of intentions. Honestly, if I am being completely real with you, that is where I lived.

Why? I am not exactly sure, but some of it probably had to do with my view of the reality of sin in our world and the likely future obliteration of our planet at the end of time. I was raised in the 1960s and 1970s, in the era of *The Late Great Planet Earth* book and movie, which likely factored into my view of the future and the reality of the present.

Before I go further, however, I want to explain just a bit more of my personal journey, as I think it will be helpful as you read this book.

I have been fortunate to have had some wonderful spiritual parenting influences in my life. My dad and mom were Baptist pastors who raised my two brothers and sister and me in a godly home in Southern California, where Jesus was the center of our lives. Even when church life was rough, I never doubted that the Lord held us in His hand. My dad had a strong evangelistic gift, and I will never forget the countless number of people in my childhood and youth whom I got to see come to know Jesus.

We also had really wonderful pastors and leaders around our home from my earliest days all through my adolescence. My dad encouraged us to experience the Jesus People movement in the 1960s and '70s, and I got to watch the activity of the Lord through Calvary Chapel Costa Mesa and Pastor Chuck Smith.

I received a call to pastoral ministry in my midteens, married Pam in my late teens and was pleased to serve in local churches and in broader missional efforts in Southern California for the first eighteen years of our marriage, where Pam and I had four of our five children.

In my midtwenties and thirties, while I was a young pastor and missional leader, several pastor friends spoke into my life. At Fuller Seminary, I was privileged to have Dr. C. Peter Wagner as one of my professors, and I got to attend a couple of sessions of his now-famous "MC510 Signs and Wonders" course with John Wimber. In this course, along with some experiences in my local church, I came to experience and believe in the power of God to heal.

Eventually I found my way to some of Pastor Jack Hayford's pastors' conferences, and I heard him speak about the voice and present work of the Holy Spirit in a refreshingly natural fashion.

In the late 1990s I came across the writings of Dr. Ed Silvoso regarding prayer, the marketplace and the *ekklesia*. (We will talk more about the concept of *ekklesia*—individuals and groups gathered as the Church—starting in the very next chapter.) Ed's writings reinforced in me the notion that the Church needs not to be a "holy huddle" but to engage and shape the world with the light of Christ.

Some of my personal ministry strengths that were evident in the 1980s, regarding civic connections between the Church and the community, blossomed even further as I began to focus more and more on the Church discovering and using spiritual gifts for ministry impact, and on identifying the marketplace as a key place of assignment.

God prospered the ministries in which Pam and I served, and I served as a senior leader in an 85-year-old Baptist church, led a large mission agency in my early thirties, and then planted a church in my midthirties. Each time we experienced growth and community impact. And again, Pam and I felt the kindness and grace of the Lord even as we navigated very challenging financial and family strains.

By the time I hit my forties, however, I had to come to grips with yet another pain-filled recognition. I was successful in many ways in pastoral ministry with church growth, speaking, writing and consulting. I was blessed with the gift of an amazing and deeply biblically grounded wife and five beautiful children. But I had been hiding a secret that was unknown even to me: *I had come to the place where I believed that God would love me more if I did more things for Him.*

Some call this an "orphan spirit"—see, for example, Jack Frost's book *Spiritual Slavery to Spiritual Sonship*—and I had it all over me without even knowing it.

Thankfully Pam and I were able to go through an inner healing ministry, "Restoring the Foundations." Several of our leadership team went through the ministry as well. The Lord brought freedom and grace to me in a new fashion. By no means did I become perfect, but I experienced a fresh wave of the love and grace of the Lord; and Pam and I have been able to share with others His healing grace that has continued in our lives.

During this season I also began leaning into a greater understanding of the presence of the Lord. Bill Johnson and Kris Vallotton, senior leaders at Bethel Church in Redding, California, became great teachers for Pam and me from a distance—and later, for me, in an ongoing and deeply meaningful relationship with Kris—as we learned about how God is speaking to us and working in our everyday lives. I began to share more widely in evangelical and charismatic streams of the Church about what I called "presence-filled ministry."

Part of what I learned and shared was that I had often led people to fulfill the purposes of God but not to enjoy just being with Him. I had to repent of that and have some painful conversations with key leaders in our Church, and admit to it publicly, which I did several times. It was during this whole process that I discovered that I really did not believe the part of the Lord's Prayer that I mentioned at the beginning of this chapter.

History, Grace, Truth

So, back to my reality of not actually believing the words on the pages of Scripture.

To be frank, I am not saying that I did not believe the Bible. I assented intellectually to the words, but without any real expectation that Jesus actually meant what He said. Ugh! I am so sorry to have to write these words, but they are true.

It was through listening to Bill and Kris and being in the Bethel atmosphere that the Holy Spirit began to tug consistently on my heart about what I believed about the phrase *on earth as it is in heaven.* Did I really believe that Jesus intended the Father's will could be done in this way? Could it be an intellectual and experiential reality that God would want earth to look like heaven? If so, was it even possible with flawed and failing human beings like me and like the people in churches that I had led, loved and lived in over the years? How could we actually see this happen? Could it be that followers of Jesus might really bring heaven to earth?

The more I began to listen and learn anew what the Holy Spirit was saying in His Word, the more I came to the conviction that the Father does indeed intend for those followers of His Son to be filled with and empowered by His Spirit and to bring life, hope, grace, peace and power to the inhabitants of the earth. We who are followers of Jesus are made for mission, and that mission happens in the everyday of life.

What you have just read, I have never said or written in a public setting at any time—and I speak and write publicly virtually every day of my life. So thank you for letting me share some of the story behind the story.

And now I have some things that I think the Lord has been preparing me for a lifetime to share with you, so we can walk this journey together.

> "Your kingdom come, your will be done, on earth as it is in heaven."
>
> Matthew 6:10

> Words create worlds.
>
> Rabbi Abraham
> Joshua Heschel[1]

Ours is a challenging moment. History matters. Grace matters. Truth matters. Yet we are living in a crisis of truth. We have moved from an acceptance of absolute truth to an understanding of relative truth. We live in the age of experiential reality, where "my truth" is relative to you but absolute to me. My experience of reality is what defines my truth. Many believe something along the lines of "You must decide to accept me and my truth or, at least in my eyes, you are mean and condemning and judgmental."

Further, the "metaverse" of virtual reality and artificial reality is cascading upon us in ways we may not fully comprehend. Words that have carried the freight of great meaning and value in previous times seem to have lost some of their impact in our contemporary world of shifting truth, evident in what were once commonly understood words. We want to believe in concepts of dignity, honor, purpose, value and community. But our lived reality is often far from our previous understanding of those words. The conflict in our hearts and minds between what we say, what we believe and what we experience seems greater than ever before.

History matters. Grace matters. Truth matters.

In our present age, the words we use have created a world that is neither what we say we believe in, nor what we have to offer the people we know, love and spend time with—and even those with whom we disagree. Social media, social unrest, pandemics of violence and health have all served to separate us from one another, to the extent that families, neighbors and community members are at odds with one another and isolated physically, socially and emotionally.

Often the truths we have taught, the history we have lived and the worldviews we express diverge sadly from the reality we live. We must shift the narrative of our words and behaviors to align with the expressed will of the Father.

I am not pessimistic about this age. In fact, with increasing fervor, I know we are in a *Go!* Season, and unless the Church is activated for this time and place, we will miss the opportunity of a lifetime.

Let me be bold and clear: The Father longs to bring heaven to earth. In fact, He has called you and me to become "grace ambassadors" in everyday life. You are called to be part of a movement to distribute grace. You are called to become an ambassador of grace here on planet earth on behalf of the King of the universe.

The first Reformation produced a cultural shift of seismic proportions on the planet. The 1500s through the 1600s produced massive intellectual, cultural and economic changes that continue to affect the world hundreds of years later. Shifts in the distribution of knowledge, patterns of governance and populist movements—often messy and venturing into uncharted waters—spread across Europe, and eventually across the globe, changing the course of history.

The Father longs to bring heaven to earth. In fact, He has called us to become "grace ambassadors" in everyday life.

Reformers are people who see the world and dream and work toward making it better and more just. The truths of the Reformation created a whole new world of change and opportunity for the masses. Words create worlds. Truth matters.

The first Reformation is still changing history and culture. It came about largely through the invention of the movable type printing press by Johannes Gutenberg in 1450—"an invention that changed the world."[2] The printing press, as you likely know, caused the words of the Bible to be spread not only in Latin but in the verbiage of the people. History matters.

The distribution of Scripture brought about the dynamic changes in history that we know as the first Reformation. History was infused with a fresh understanding and release of grace so that the Church and culture alike could receive the blessing of salvation by grace through faith in the cross of Christ. That blessing of grace would be made manifest throughout culture as newly empowered people began to think, create, develop and reimagine a world that had previously been unthinkable and unattainable. Grace matters.

But now the fading influence of that first Reformation has created a longing and increasing hunger for more of what God has for us in our present age. This longing is emerging from deep in the soul of the human experience. The Body of Christ has experienced one Reformation, but the world has lost its bearings and is in desperate need of a second Reformation. You, my precious reader, are the key to the revival that is in the heart of God for this hour.

Your Future History

I believe the King of the universe is calling you to a heavenly ambassadorship beyond your wildest dreams! You are not a bit player. You are not, to use a sports analogy, someone riding the bench. You are on the floor, on the field and in the battle. You are a difference-maker, a vibrant and vital part of His people here on planet earth. You have an identity, an assignment and an opportunity to shift the future of our planet. Much lies ahead of you, and bringing heaven to earth is a life purpose that will catalyze your life here and now, bring calling from above and establish your trajectory for all eternity.

> *I believe the King of the universe is calling you to a heavenly ambassadorship beyond your wildest dreams!*

I am writing this book because, although for a long time I did not believe it was possible, I now have a passion to see heaven come to earth. The love and grace of Jesus can transform our personal lives and the lives of our families, organizations and communities through the revival that is on God's heart. I have grown to understand that the Father has placed His people in various settings in culture and society, all with stories full of intrigue and uncertainty, in order to accomplish His purposes on the planet. You are being called not just to live in history, but to make history.

Life is experienced in video and remembered in snapshots. I imagine you have quite a few snapshots of the story of your life so far. Sometimes those snapshots are full of joy and sometimes they are full of pain. But in total, those snapshots have helped shape who you are today.

And your future is full of amazing snapshots and videos! In fact, Ephesians 2:8–10 gives us a glimpse of the reality of our salvation by grace and that we are "to do good works, which God prepared in advance for us to do." You have a life story that is only now unfolding.

I am writing this book to give you snapshots of the "future history" that you are called to but that you have not yet lived. These snapshots of your calling will lead you to a dynamic future that you can barely imagine. I am trusting God and believing that a revival and reformation will happen in your future history as you live out the story that your heavenly Father has designed for you.

How did that first Reformation come to pass?

First Reformation

On October 31, 1517, an obscure Catholic priest named Martin Luther strode up to the castle church at Wittenberg, Germany, and nailed his *Ninety-Five Theses* to the door.

Thus, the first historical Reformation of the Church began out of the crisis of one man observing the gap between what the Word of God revealed and what he was experiencing in his own life as a Catholic priest. This crisis led Luther to the extreme decision of drawing a line in the sand, nailing his complaints to the Church door and, in turn, shaping his own historic times.

In that first Reformation, Protestantism was launched with the five "*solas*"—Latin statements summarizing five core biblical beliefs: People are saved by grace alone, through faith alone, in Christ alone, as revealed by Scripture alone, to the glory of God alone. These *solas* were communicated through Gutenberg's printing press across the Western world.

Because much of the Church had allowed corruption to enter the system, reforms about salvation, access to Scripture, access to forgiveness and the clarity of theological teaching were established and strengthened in that first Reformation. The truths of doctrine and teaching were expounded and undergirded, and people were catechized into these understandings. Words matter. Truth matters.

The reformers also said they believed in the priesthood of all believers with direct access to God, to Scripture and to ministry. As the apostle Peter wrote,

> You are a chosen people, a royal priesthood, a holy nation, God's special possession, that you may declare the praises of him who called you out of darkness into his wonderful light.
>
> 1 Peter 2:9

But although glorious ministry has come these past five hundred years, the Church today has demonstrated by our behavior that we do not fundamentally believe in the priesthood of all believers. **Rather, we practice a big view of** *grace received* **and a small view of** *grace distributed.* We say that heaven came to earth in Jesus, but we do not really live as though heaven is present here. Rather, we have maintained religious hierarchy to such a degree that, for more than five hundred years, the divide between clergy and laity has become seemingly unbridgeable.

The effect of our lived and demonstrated belief is a disengaged mass of people who have tasted of Jesus in religious settings but have not been discipled toward spiritual maturity, reproduction and heavenly ambassadorship. To be frank, most spiritual leaders would have to admit that, generally speaking, we have produced babies and sons and daughters, but alarmingly few fathers and mothers in the faith (see 1 John 2:12–14). Our world stands in need of revival and reformation.

Grace distributed is the mandate of this hour for the people of God.

But as we learn to bring heaven to earth and distribute the grace of God in everyday life, we will experience the return of New Testament Christianity. This is how we will see the second Reformation birthed in our time.

Second Reformation

God has been at work in recent decades, and I believe the second Reformation is now upon us. *Grace distributed* is the mandate of this hour for the people of God.

Billy Graham believed that laypersons were the key to evangelism. Toward the end of the twentieth century, we saw the rise of apostolic and prophetic networks and the rise of interdenominational movements like Full Gospel Business Men's Fellowship, Concerned Women for America, the Jesus People movement, Promise Keepers and TheCall. The political disequilibrium of 2010–2020 and the pandemic of 2020–2022 have provided a fertile context for the emergence of the second Reformation. The future of the Church is unfolding, and the Bible describes and calls for the five-fold ministry gifts (which we will discuss in more detail in chapter 5):

> Christ himself gave the apostles, the prophets, the evangelists, the pastors and teachers, to equip his people for works of service, so that the body of Christ may be built up until we all reach unity in the faith and in the knowledge of the Son of God and become mature, attaining to the whole measure of the fullness of Christ.
>
> Ephesians 4:11–13

The Church must establish, equip, release and shepherd tens of millions of believers to influence society for the glory of God, through bringing heaven to earth and distributing grace, full of the life and love of Jesus. Everyday men and women, empowered by the Holy Spirit, will reach people in everyday life so we see the "billion soul harvest" that many have been praying and trusting God for in recent years.[3] History matters.

The first Reformation changed Western culture and provided the seedbed for the Renaissance and the Age of Enlightenment. The social changes coming from those two movements shaped not only hundreds of years of history but life on the planet. The second Reformation will bring about even greater societal transformation as followers of Jesus are activated in love, grace, redemptive presence and dynamic Kingdom witness to the good news of the presence of Jesus for men and women longing for hope and meaning in life.

The greatest days of Gospel ministry are emerging in this new Reformation, and each of us has a part to play in the divine orchestra that Jesus is directing. It is indeed *Go!* time for Spirit-empowered followers of Jesus to manifest the grace of heaven on earth in everyday settings so we can see revival and reformation at home, at church and in the culture. Grace matters.

Understanding the grace of God, receiving that grace and becoming part of bringing heaven to earth as a grace distributor in your everyday life are Kingdom mandates and your "future history" assignment. Even today as you live your life, you are beginning to sense that you were made for more.

In fact, there has been an increasing heart cry for *more* across the Body of Christ. Political divisions and pandemic anxieties have increased the uncertainty that many in our world experience, with even followers of Jesus unclear about the future. Pentecost brought 120 believers to a Spirit of God encounter that would go on to transform the Roman empire and set the course for Western and world history. How did a Church so full of the power of God and clarity about personal assignment lose her way? What is the condition of the Church today, and how can we move to the calling of the Father to be heavenly grace distributors in this moment?

Read on and let the Spirit speak to your heart, mind and spirit.

BEFORE YOU GO

Think for a moment about words that have been spoken in your life. Do you remember any life-giving words? Do you remember any words that felt condemning or judgmental? How did the words of your memories end up affecting your personal history? How have you experienced the grace and kindness of God to make your life fuller and more complete?

2

CHRISTIAN LIFE IN THE NOW

As a child, James attended church regularly with his family. It always seemed exciting when the church gathered together. The games in the classes with the other kids were fun. Food was often provided, and the adults who gathered around him were a welcome breath of happiness—a far cry from his home situation, where his parents fought about financial and social pressures he did not understand.

By the time James was a teenager, church attendance was less frequent for the whole family. James attended only when his mother nagged him to do so. While James still liked several of the kids at church, the gap between his family reality and that of the other church families seemed too great to bridge.

High school graduation brought new freedoms, including the choice to stop attending church except for special occasions. James attended church only on holidays—typically Christmas and Easter and occasionally on Mother's Day— throughout his early twenties.

The Christian faith today is often lifeless and disengaged from public culture. Particularly in first world settings, many find their spiritual lives just a helpful accessory to a social fabric already full of material comfort. The contrast between first world and third world spirituality is often stark and challenging. Many first world followers of Jesus experience a convenient form of spiritual life with little engagement with neighbors, little connection to popular culture and infrequent experiences of the power of God demonstrated in their personal lives or cultural settings. Our personal experience with Jesus, perhaps shared with a few people in church, has little to no effect on the culture of our communities.

The seeming success of many megachurches (including a few I was privileged to lead) have lulled many to sleep. This apparent success often looks like an earthly definition of success with little evidence of the movement, miracles and ministry of heaven. And it has come as the public culture around us has run headlong from the core of Gospel truth.

Even a surface examination of the Christian life today suggests that the Gospel is incapable of producing societal change and reformation. We declare many things with power but have little experience of actually seeing the power of God change a human life, family, organization or community. We have a lot of earth on earth, but precious little of heaven on earth. I think during the past decades that the Lord has been giving His people a massive wakeup call, but we have yet to respond in large measure to His promptings for the longings of heaven.

I have the privilege of being a father to three daughters and two sons. As I write this today, I fondly remember the wedding preparations for each of my three daughters. So many details! So many aspects to the preparations that I did not understand, even though I had been a pastor all my life!

Each of my daughters and their husbands had the bride-and-groom experience of a wedding within the limits of our budget but appropriate for their personalities. Each of our daughters was a radiant and beautiful bride (yes, I am biased!); and my wife, the mother of the bride, was gloriously adorned on each occasion. The weddings of my daughters were exhilarating and exhausting; they were radiant brides, and the "work" of being radiant was evidenced in the experience and photographs and memories of the events.

Scripture uses the imagery of the Church as the radiant Bride of Christ, to be presented "without spot or wrinkle" (Ephesians 5:27 ESV). This imagery is a challenge for many of us as we think about how we experience church. But the Bride of Christ was never meant to be a retiring and reticent creature of comfort. Bringing heaven to earth is the work of His love and grace for the planet. The Church is to be strategic, forward-leaning and fully engaged. We are not called to be isolated and detached from the world around us. Just the opposite. The Church is to overcome the realm of darkness that has been exercising dominion over this rebellious planet since the moment of the Fall in the Garden.

Being the Bride of Christ, then, is no passive spectator experience. Brides are actively engaged in the fulfillment of their roles—a wonderful experience but hard work. And the Church is to be the best Bride of all time!

Sadly, some of us in the global Church have subscribed to one of several belief systems that have corrupted our engagement with society and turned us aside from our God-given commission to be grace ambassadors. Let's look at three of these.

1. The Watchmaker/Blueprint Worldview

The first belief system that we in the global Church have accommodated ourselves to is a variation of the "watchmaker theory"—the belief that the purpose and complexity of a watch found lying on the sand would imply the existence of a watchmaker. In the same way, some believers assume that God wound up the universe like a watch, setting in motion the course of events that would ultimately come to pass. Human free will, according to this worldview, has little to do with affecting real history on the planet. Fatalism and cultural detachment are the natural results of this worldview.

But the clear and compelling story of Scripture is that God partners with individuals and groups of people gathered as the Church (or *ekklesia*) to accomplish His Kingdom purposes on earth. In fact, Scripture tells us that we have the honor of representing the King in sharing His love with others.

First John 4:19 says that "we love because he first loved us." And 2 Corinthians 5:19–21 (TLB) tells us that

> God was in Christ, restoring the world to himself, no longer counting men's sins against them but blotting them out. This is the wonderful message he has given us to tell others. We are Christ's ambassadors. God is using us to speak to you: we beg you, as though Christ himself were here pleading with you, receive the love he offers you—be reconciled to God. For God took the sinless Christ and poured into him our sins. Then, in exchange, he poured God's goodness into us!

We who have been greatly loved have the opportunity to share His love with others. We in the household of faith who celebrate the grace we have received have the opportunity to share that grace with others. Sadly, however, many of us have lost our passion to be ambassadors of the high King of heaven to bring heaven to earth and be distributors of His grace to others. We have lost our redemptive heartbeat and lack the passion to reach others with the same love and grace that reached us.

Let's remember the founding story of what it means to be part of the Bride of Christ. The return of Jesus to planet earth, first as a Babe in the manger and second as conquering King, is the greatest rescue story ever told. Jesus came to save, heal and deliver from darkness and oppression those who have been captured by the enemy of their souls. The fundamental mission of the Church is to live "to the praise of his glorious grace" (Ephesians 1:6) by being ambassadors of reconciliation in the world (see 2 Corinthians 5:18–21) and "[making] disciples of all nations" (Matthew 28:19) through the equipping of the saints through the fivefold ministry of Ephesians 4:11–13.

Remember that we talked in chapter 1 about the fivefold ministry: apostles, prophets, evangelists, pastors and teachers. Each of these dimensions is foundational to New Testament Christianity. When we live out our mission, we will bring heaven on earth in the communities and everyday settings where God has assigned us, individually and corporately.

Although many of us know these things, however, an alarmingly small number of us have actually experienced the overflow of Kingdom life as the Bride of Christ, the global Church. Instead of being an activist and activated Church, many of us have defaulted to the watchmaker or blueprint view—believing that we have little to do with changing history on our planet, since God has already determined what will happen—and we have little to no engagement in society. We often satisfy ourselves with our gatherings of insiders, with little passion for reaching those outside the family of believers.

The destructive reality of this worldview has been the experience and demonstration of a gospel that is largely impotent to reach and transform culture. We have developed our own satisfaction with the personal effects of our proximity to Jesus but negated His imperative to teach and disciple the nations. This worldview and behavior pattern have caused tremendous damage to our world.

Dr. George Barna and his research associates have been studying worldview for close to thirty years. Here are just a few of their assessments of the spiritual condition of the Church (largely reflective of first world Christianity).

In 2015, 87 percent of millennials surveyed by the Barna Group who did not attend church believed that Christians were judgmental, while 85 percent believed Christians were hypocritical.[1] Equally troubling is that in the same 2015 Barna survey, 66 percent of millennials who *did* attend church believed that Christians are hypocritical.[2]

Barna's 2021 "Millennials in America" survey found that only 2 percent of millennials ages 18–24 had a biblical worldview even though 65 percent of them claimed to be Christian.[3] This survey quotes earlier reports:

> In virtually every study we conduct, representing thousands of interviews every year, born-again Christians fail to display much attitudinal or behavioral evidence of transformed lives. For instance, based on a study released in 2007, we found that most of the lifestyle activities of born-again Christians were statistically equivalent to those of non-born. When asked to identify their activities over the last thirty day, born-again believers were just as likely to bet or gamble, to visit a pornographic website, to take something that did not belong to them, to consult a medium or psychic, to physically fight or abuse someone, to have consumed enough alcohol to be considered legally drunk, to have used an illegal, nonprescription

drug, to have said something to someone that was not true, to have gotten back at someone for something he or she did and to have said mean things behind another person's back. No difference.[4]

How to account for this lack of evidence of transformation? The following short history of Christianity is attributed to Richard Halverson, former chaplain of the U.S. Senate:

In the beginning the church was a fellowship of men and women centering on the living Christ. Then the church moved to Greece, where it became a philosophy. Then it moved to Rome, where it became an institution. Next, it moved to Europe, where it became a culture. And, finally, it moved to America, where it became an enterprise.[5]

Finally comes this observation from Os Guinness, Christian author and social critic:

The problem with Christians in America is not that Christians aren't where they should be; the problem is that they're not what they should be right where they are.[6]

Many observers believe that the European continent is about fifty years "ahead" of the United States in terms of religious decline. While we see some signs of the stirrings of revival in Africa, South America and Asia, we still have not seen the transformational impact in our time that we witnessed in the book of Acts and in previous global movements of the Church.

How did we arrive at such a place? We hear of large churches and growing ministries in some areas, but a simultaneous, tragic lack of alignment as to righteousness and cultural impact. Why is it that so many cultural contexts, in which a Christian worldview was once woven into the national fabric, have now become frayed? Why is the Church so systematically disengaged from the public square and seemingly accepting of abandoning culture without a redemptive moral compass? Our declining influence is evident in the political and social realms of culture.

Many who formerly identified as "evangelical" have now shed that label. Others have begun to press in further to deeply understand our role in the created world rather than accept the fatalistic underpinnings of the watchmaker/blueprint worldview. I personally have been grappling with Jesus' words when He said, through the words of a parable, that we are to "occupy till I come" (Luke 19:13 KJV).

How do we do this? And how did we come to satisfy ourselves with grace received while defaulting on our compelling obligation and opportunity to be part of grace distributed? Why are we satisfied with earth on earth when we are called to bring and manifest heaven on earth?

2. The Sacred/Secular Divide

In addition to the watchmaker/blueprint worldview, much of the global Church has been the victim of another belief system that has corrupted our engagement with society: our acceptance of the sacred/secular divide.

This worldview accepts the notion that human existence is divided into two spheres. The sphere of church and religious activity is sacred, and everything else is secular. This view has allowed many in the Church to pursue religious affection (or at least religious activity) divorced from cultural engagement. Sadly, we have abandoned entire generations to a culture dominated by varying forms of hedonism, humanism and secularism, without a vibrant Kingdom of God presence and witness. This worldview split is a cancer in the Church and must be confronted.

Years ago I was struck by Pastor Terry Crist in his book *Learning the Language of Babylon: Changing the World by Engaging the Culture*:

> Several years ago, in a time of intense soul-searching, the Lord asked me this startling question: Who gave you the right to bargain off my property? Though it was a simple question, it produced a major paradigm shift in my thinking. In a moment of revelation, I felt I understood the purpose behind the question. Like many others, I had sat down at that table of unilateral disarmament with the enemy and said to him, in effect, "Don't bother us and we won't bother you! You can have the kingdoms of this world—entertainment, the arts, media, politics, athletics, law, economics—and we will take our Sunday school programs, Bible clubs, Christian conferences and home Bible studies. If you leave us alone, we'll leave you alone."[7]

Not only did Crist share his personal revelation moment about the consequences of his sacred/secular mindset; he also began to dig into history, where he discovered a series of strong teachings confronting this destructive and bifurcated worldview. Crist discovered Abraham Kuyper, a theologian, journalist and prime minister of the Netherlands at the beginning of the twentieth century. In Kuyper's inaugural address at the Free University of Amsterdam (which he founded) on October 20, 1880, he challenged the withdrawal of the Church from the public sector:

> There is not one square inch in the whole domain of our human existence over which Christ, who is Sovereign over all, does not cry: "Mine!"[8]

This lecture formed the basis for Kuyper's teaching on "sphere sovereignty," in which he identified seven basic areas of life, each possessing its own sovereignty or authority: government, family, religion, business, education, science and the arts.

Kuyper's views were to affect broad swaths of the Body of Christ, and are currently found across evangelical, charismatic and fundamentalist streams of the Church. The "seven mountains" movement in the modern era—popularized by Francis Schaeffer, Bill Bright and Loren Cunningham in the 1970s, and more recently by Lance Wallnau and others—comes directly from Kuyper's challenge.

I believe the sacred/secular divide to be a particularly toxic form of thinking. It has prevented the priesthood of all believers—the reality from 1 Peter 2:9 that we looked at in the last chapter—from taking place, as it encourages pastors to be in charge of the "sacred" and those not in full-time pastoral ministry to consider their vocation "secular."

I contend that God is calling for a second Reformation in which we actually live out the Great Commission and disciple nations in every sphere of society. How? By learning to bring heaven to earth and being distributors of grace as heavenly ambassadors.

God is calling for a second Reformation in which we actually live out the Great Commission and disciple nations in every sphere of society.

Discipling, equipping and releasing the people of God to Kingdom ministry across cultures will be the foundational activity in the second Reformation. I believe we are on the edge of that Reformation even now. Can you imagine thousands (millions!) of believers all over the planet being the presence of

Christ and fulfilling the Great Commission every day in their families and neighborhoods and workplaces?

We have received grace; now we need to learn to distribute it with a compelling and engaging love. The love we have received by God's grace is the love that compels us to be distributors of His grace so that we can help others come to know the same forgiveness and freedom.

3. Extreme Eschatology

One final belief system that we will discuss has corrupted the engagement of the global Church with society, and that is our eschatology—the theology of last things, our view of how the world will end.

Around the year 1900, an extreme expression of millennialism (referring to Jesus' reign during the Millennium) taught that He was coming back immediately. In fact, Jesus' return was so imminent that people canceled long-term plans and stopped investing in generation-spanning efforts. The destructive streams of culture were actually confirmations, they believed, of the impending Rapture, Tribulation and millennial reign of Christ. They saw culture as the revelation of a world heading toward a cataclysmic end with no potential for redemption. The Church was powerless to change this trajectory. In fact, it was actually the fulfillment of a prophetic order that had been decreed and was being lived out.

I have many friends in the premillennial camp who believe very strongly that Christians will be rescued before any form of tribulation. They are clear about the destruction that will happen on the planet even before the Tribulation and ultimate millennial period.

I personally have no certainty regarding the exact timing and details of the return of Jesus Christ. But I have become increasingly concerned about the effects of what I term "extreme eschatology" on our ecclesiology. By this I mean that our eschatology is often "upstream" of our ecclesiology (our view of the Church both gathered and scattered). In simple terms, our extreme focus on eschatology has often resulted in a diminished burden for people outside the household of faith. I think flawed eschatology produces ecclesiology without a redemptive heartbeat.

Even some followers of Jesus who do not align with a premillennial view believe that the social and cultural wars are already lost, and that Christians should retreat to varied forms of isolation and try to rebuild society in small, clustered contexts. As one example, let me highlight the writings of Rod Dreher.

I have deep appreciation for Dreher's work in *The Benedict Option: A Strategy for Christians in a Post-Christian Nation* and *Live Not by Lies: A Manual for Christian Dissidents*. My argument is not with the content of his books but with their application by some of his readers. Any expectation of future events that causes followers of Christ to disengage from the world is missing the fundamental nature of Father, Son and Holy Spirit as Redeemer. The love of God is a redeeming love and needs to be experienced and understood in that light.

No matter what our view or chronology of end-time events, it is critical that the Church engage with the culture. The reason God left us on the planet is to testify to His goodness and grace and to live to the praise of His glory as we bring heaven to earth. Since God is a redeeming God, we who love Him are compelled to testify of His love and live and work redemptively for the sake of the world. The cultural mandate to bring about heaven on earth is both a response to Jesus' own prayer and a present participation in His work.

Proclaiming the Gospel for eternal salvation is our first responsibility. But I do not believe it is our last.

But this view is not universally accepted in the Church. Dave Hunt, the Christian apologist and author, for example, advocates against Christian activism. He wrote:

> "Christian activism" is not Christian. It represents a detour from the straight path the Church is to walk before the world. It can confuse the real issues, lead to compromise and unholy alliances and divert time and effort that would better be used in proclaiming the gospel. Weigh the demands upon your time and set priorities. Be fully engaged in rescuing souls for eternity.[9]

I agree that we must proclaim the gospel of forgiveness, but I believe the gospel of forgiveness is only a partial gospel. The Gospel of Jesus Christ includes forgiveness, healing and deliverance. When Jesus prayed that the will of God "be done on earth as it is in heaven," He was proclaiming both intent and assignment. We who carry the life of the Risen One, empowered by the same Spirit who raised Jesus from the dead, have the assignment, authority and power to manifest and extend the Kingdom of God in every domain we encounter.

Os Hillman, president of Marketplace Leaders and internationally recognized speaker on the subject of faith at work, is a powerful advocate for this worldview I am describing. Listen to his encouragement here:

> Making disciples of entire people groups and nations is the end game. It is thrilling to consider that the cry "Thy kingdom come. Thy will be done on earth, as it is in heaven" makes heaven available through you right now to potentially fix whatever is broken in any earthly system you are assigned

to. This is God's desire. In the end the leaves of the tree of life are "for the healing of nations."[10]

Prevailing against the Darkness

As we close this chapter, I want to share a profound encouragement that I received on what cultural transformation can look like and how it often takes place.

It has become too easy—due in part to three worldviews we have explored in this chapter—to see cultural decay as a natural result of the approaching end times and the unstoppable decadence of our culture. I say no to that view of our future! The Church is called to be an agent of transformation and to prevail against the darkness of our world. So read these words and be encouraged. In the next chapter we will start to unpack more fully what Scripture says to us about our mandate in the here and now.

We have discussed the redemptive heartbeat of God; the call of Jesus for us to be salt and light in the world; His exhortation for us not to lose our saltiness or let our light be hidden (see Matthew 5:13–16); and His call for us to disciple nations and teach them to obey all He has commanded (see Matthew 28:18–20). **Any view of Christian obedience that does not see believers engaging with culture and seeking to save the lost, heal the sick, and disciple the saved is not in alignment with the biblical missional mandate of the Church.** Throughout history the Church has understood her mission as such, and has manifested that missional focus in cultural transformation, particularly in the Western world.[11]

Much of the modern Church, however, has been retreating from culture. The "polarity" of the world has changed and we have not recognized it. Polarity—positive and negative electrical current—has understood properties and effects in the natural world. In the same way, we may still expect family, church and school to contain a moral compass and to shape and filter culture accordingly. But today the polarity has shifted. Media and schools and corporations now shape individuals and families with very little moral filtering or alignment.

The people of God in this generation, then, must learn to become atmosphere changers as part of our spiritual battle (see Ephesians 6) as we shift the cultural institutions in our world.

James Hunter, distinguished educator and senior fellow at the Trinity Forum, wrote in his book *To Change the World*:

> Imagine . . . a genuine "third great awakening" occurring in America, where half of the population is converted to a deep Christian faith. Unless this awakening extended to envelop the cultural gatekeepers, it would have little effect on the character of the symbols that are produced and prevail in public and private culture. And, without a fundamental restructuring of the institutions of culture formation and transmission in our society—the market, government-sponsored cultured institutions, education at all levels, advertising, entertainment, publishing and the news media, not to mention Church—revival would have a negligible long-term effect on the reconstitution of the culture.[12]

All this may seem rather complex. Really it is simple. If we see revival limited to church gatherings, culture will not change, especially if we retain the sacred/secular divide. Only when people come to know Jesus, receive His glorious grace, and live and love in society as a redemptive force for Him will we see cultural transformation. Revival reforms culture. "When the righteous thrive, the people rejoice; when the wicked rule, the people groan" (Proverbs 29:2).

Now is the time for the people of God to seize the opportunity and mandate as His people to see God's Kingdom come and His will to "be done on earth as it is in heaven." This is the Father's will.

The second Reformation is here, and it looks like bringing heaven to earth. Distributing His grace in everyday life is an opportunity for us to see revival, transformation and reformation.

But first we must understand how we got to this place. The next chapter will help us understand.

BEFORE YOU GO

Spend a few moments to reflect on your experience with "church." Did you grow up in church? Do you have happy or sad or frustrating or joyous emotions about your experiences in church? Did you connect with God and with people through your church? When you think of your relationship with God, has church helped you deepen the intimacy of your connection with Him, or not? Do you maintain a sense of mission and assignment when you are away from the church building? Do you experience the world any differently from your friends who are not part of a church community?

3

HOW DID WE GET HERE?

James met Rebecca when they were both 24. They worked in the same office and discovered over time that they shared similar interests and backgrounds. Rebecca was not a person of faith, but she had been to church a few times. When James and Rebecca got married, having the ceremony in church seemed the right thing, particularly to be sensitive to James's parents, who, although they did not attend church regularly anymore, did still attend on holidays with James and his siblings.

James and Rebecca followed a similar sporadic church attendance pattern until the birth of their first child. The stress of the pregnancy and reading about child development made them wonder if they needed a community to help them teach values to their baby boy.

But along with the birth of the new baby came busy days and sleep-deprived nights. Church never really happened until their toddler turned three and started asking challenging questions he must have learned at preschool. Their search

*for a church where they could learn about teaching values
without becoming too religious began in earnest.*

How did the Church become a cultural curiosity and annoyance instead of a source of cultural origin, blessing, pride and transformation? Rather than for us to languish in a pool of despair, I long for us to seize the day and move to the future that the Father waits to give birth to within and through us.

Followers of Jesus have a mandate to create the future because of our hope in Him, which is the hope of heaven. Even when the people of God were scattered because of persecution, the apostles challenged them to cling to their hope and peace in Jesus, whose resurrection is the evidence of our salvation (see 1 Peter 1:1–9). As people with "confidence in what we hope for and assurance about what we do not see" (Hebrews 11:1), we say no to despair and yes to hope.

Yet even while we make these declarations of hope, we recognize the reality of the present circumstances. The time has come for us in the household of faith to have a frank conversation about the status of the Church and her relationship to culture.

My friend Sam Rodriguez, an anointed prophetic leader, often says, "Today's complacency is tomorrow's captivity." The Church around the world has lived out that prophetic word for the past seven or more decades—the entire course of my life. The results, particularly in first world cultures, have been devastating for Gospel witness. I am writing this book, then, out of a sense of urgency for the Church, the people of God, to live into what our loving Father so desires for us to experience and then manifest to others.

Sadly for me as an American, many international friends tell me that the American Church that was once a model for them to emulate has become a mission field for them to reach. Not only does this pain my heart, but it stirs up longing in me to see the grace and love and power of God released and distributed through His people in cultural settings across the globe, wherever He has assigned us. Heaven on earth comes when we manifest the life of Jesus through the power of the Spirit.

Much of what the Church has manifested these past decades has been a gospel without the power of God to transform lives. The statistics and critiques I cited in the last chapter provide a baseline for the often apathetic and detached condition of much of the Church in the first world.

I have no comprehensive framework for why and how the Church across the globe has had a declining moral influence at various times in our shared experience. I know enough of history to realize that there have been moments—for example, in a U.S. context, before the American Revolution; before the second Great Awakening; and during the pre-1900s and mid-1900s—when the spiritual condition of America was particularly bad, and cultural degradations particularly challenging and disturbing. But each time the culture seemed on the edge of destruction, God sent a move: the First and Second Great Awakenings, the Welsh revival, Azusa Street, the Jesus People, and the charismatic renewal of the 1960s, '70s and '80s. These moves brought fresh wind, fresh fire and fresh power to the people of God in the midst of cultural disequilibrium.

We say *Yes!* and *Do it again, Lord!*

Three Massive Misses

I have often pondered why certain sectors of the Church in my lifetime seem successful (for example, the rise of megachurches and the Christian media) while the moral clarity of the culture heads in the opposite direction. If the Church is successful, why has our culture been deteriorating? Some say that culture is the report card of the Church. If this is the case, we are in deep waters across the world.

This dissonance has agitated my spirit, as I am sure it has yours. Again, I say that I long to see the Bride of Christ be the redemptive force on the planet that I know is the heart of the Father.

During my seasons of pondering, I have come to recognize at least three massive "misses" that have contributed to the Church's declining influence in culture. These misses are embodied in the words *apathy*, *affluence* and *attachment*. Let's look more closely at each of these.

Apathy

Our first miss is our *apathy* about sharing our hope in Jesus. If we really believe that family members, neighbors, friends and co-workers are going to hell without Jesus, our behavior would change. I know that *my* behavior would change if that understanding were rooted in my spirit. Sometimes I have sensed the Holy Spirit convicting me about the casual nature of my relationships with people who do not know Jesus. In these relationships I lack an urgency to share the good news of salvation and freedom in Jesus.

Can you imagine having the cure for cancer and not sharing it with your family member who had cancer? It would be an unspeakable act of evil, a blot on your character. So why do we not share Jesus in a loving, compassionate and urgent fashion with those He places in our lives?

Our *apathy* about sharing Jesus comes, I believe, from the second miss.

Affluence

Our second miss is our *affluence* in first world life. We have not recognized the tremendous gift of our comfortable circumstances, providing us in Kingdom stewardship with an opportunity to testify to the goodness of God and live with the power of our testimony and be a fountain of generosity.

I am clear, from repeated lessons throughout Scripture, that wealth is not evil. Quite the contrary. Wealth is a gift from God and a resource in His Kingdom. God entrusts wealth to His children so we can live as vessels of blessing and channel His resources to His purposes, including caring for our families and the poor in our communities.

Material comfort has led many of us, however, to a place of contentment and detachment from the circumstances of our communities and those who may be suffering in plain sight all around us. In my role as a pastor and Christian university president, I see statistics about communities in which the presence of churches is strong, but the simultaneous reality of homelessness, immorality and crime is increasing. Somehow we have come to accept this as normal!

This concurrent reality of spiritual atmospheres—light and darkness together—is often obscured or accepted due to what I believe is our third and most personally painful miss.

Attachment

Our third miss is our *attachment* to an unbiblical understanding of success. The preceding two paragraphs were difficult for me to write. This paragraph feels even more personally devastating.

I have led and participated in many aspects of the evangelical church growth movement since the late 1970s. I have

shared in and encouraged many aspects of the charismatic and Pentecostal renewal since the 1980s. Many good things have come from these and other movements. In each of them, however, I believe we have equated the size of the crowd with the scope of our impact. This is terribly and tragically wrong. We have missed the mark.

We have given birth to many spiritual babies. But we have grown fewer sons and daughters, and even fewer fathers and mothers who can shepherd their flock to maturity.

While audience size has grown—more megachurches, multi-site and media-driven ministries than ever before in history—the shocking truth is that we have *not* been consistently producing disciples who surrender their lives to Jesus, are rooted in the faith and are walking in the presence and power of the Holy Spirit to reproduce new babies in the faith who grow up to be healthy, reproducing fathers and mothers. We have given birth to many spiritual babies. But we have grown fewer sons and daughters, and even fewer fathers and mothers who can shepherd their flock to maturity.

Isaiah 61 Revival

I grieve over these misses. I long to see the Bride of Christ "without spot or wrinkle" (Ephesians 5:27 ESV) walking in the power of the Holy Spirit and bringing life, hope, joy and peace to our world. I long to see an Isaiah 61 revival in which the blind see, the lame walk, captives are set free, and "oaks of righteousness" (Isaiah 61:3; see also Luke 4:16–20) are established in every community and people group, so the testimony of Jesus is released across the planet.

I do not despair, and neither should you! The pandemic of 2020–22 was a moment in which the Church was called forth and stirred up and awakened. Because of our hope in Christ, we lean in when others lean away. We are to be like the early Christians in plague-stricken Rome who stayed when others fled, who rescued babies from trash heaps and who saw the healing power of Jesus manifested in the everyday of challenging life circumstances. In fact, I believe that the present circumstances are the seedbed from which a tremendous harvest will come.

Now is the right time, perhaps more than ever in the last fifty–plus years, for the Church to realize her inheritance and bring forth the work of the King in His Kingdom. Because we believe in the Lordship of Christ, we are able to say no to fear and to lean in to the creative capacity of the Father to bring about solutions to seemingly insoluble problems.

I believe that the cure to cancer and solutions to homelessness, illegal immigration and every other social problem are in heaven waiting to be delivered to earth through the people of God.

I see a future in which the people of God determine to be salt and light, a redemptive presence on the planet with the passionate love of Jesus for the women and men, families and communities He has called us to reach. When that happens, every follower of Jesus will be part of the second Reformation, and we will see grace distributed and heaven demonstrated in every segment of society.

Before that takes place, we must understand the difference between the Church and the Kingdom of God. Understanding this difference will lead us on the path to the second Reformation.

BEFORE YOU GO

Do the three "misses" resonate with you personally? Do you think of apathy, affluence and attachment as things that may have influenced the way you interact with culture? Have you experienced seasons when you felt lulled into complacency and away from spiritual vitality? As you think about the current condition of our world, do you find yourself depressed and despairing, or are you hopeful for the future?

4

THE CHURCH
AND THE KINGDOM

James and Rebecca tried out a few churches but were initially frustrated. Some of the churches they tried were not very friendly. Others seemed as if their culture and words and social groups were all fixed in stone. But thankfully they found a church not too far from their home that seemed to fit them. James and Rebecca were drawn to the consistent teaching. The music sounded contemporary and drew them to deeper spiritual reflection.

Most interesting to them was that the church members really cared about one another and about their local community. Every week, it seemed, they were talking about the local school, about ministering to the needy in their town, or working with the city leaders to address healthcare and support the local business community.

That kind of community engagement got James and Rebecca's attention as they grappled with parenting a precocious three-year-old boy who had harder questions every day....

M y dear friend Kris Vallotton says, "All of the Church is in the Kingdom but not all of the Kingdom is in the Church."[1] Have you heard this saying before? The first time I heard it, it made perfect sense to me.

I am a lover of the Church and have been part of it since my birth. (Never missed a Sunday or Wednesday from birth through age sixteen!) I also know that Jesus came and ushered in the Kingdom of God (see, for example, Mark 1:15; Luke 8:1; 17:21; John 18:36). So how should we think about the Kingdom of God and the Church?

Let's start by defining Church as either the *oikos* (Greek for a small, extended household of faith) or the *ekklesia* (Greek for an assembly of citizens). The original use of *ekklesia* within Roman culture described a gathering of Roman citizens with the authority of their citizenship in the Empire). In the book of Acts, we read about the Church gathered ("Temple courts") and the Church distributed ("house to house" or in the marketplace). In both cases—when the Church is gathered and when the Church is distributed— she manifests the grace of the presence of God just as Jesus promised (see Matthew 18:20). The Scripture is clear that the Church gathered and the Church scattered are both the *ekklesia*.

So let's return to Kris Vallotton's statement that "all of the Church is in the Kingdom, but not all of the Kingdom is in the Church." If the Kingdom of God is everywhere that the rule and reign of God is manifested, then we understand that the boundaries of the Church gathered are starting points for the Kingdom, but not the full measure of it.

On the other hand, many of us have been lulled into a complacency that it is only what we experience in the Church gathered that constitutes the Kingdom in its totality. Our belief about the limitations of the Church, then, prevents us from experiencing the full measure of the Kingdom reality that Jesus brought to earth.

Gathered and Distributed

Our belief in the sacred/secular divide (which we discussed in chapter 2) deceives us into a worldview in which we think of the Church as "sanctified" and the society or culture as "stained." This view has had devastating consequences, which most of us have experienced in the way that the Church avoids engagement with the world. The truth is, when we are the Church distributed, in the everyday world of our lives, we are no less the Church than when we are gathered together.

Sadly, in much of our recent experience, and in many settings, we have become enamored of the gathering of the Church to the exclusion of the distribution of the Church. And to the extent that we minimize the Church distributed, we lose the missional nature of the Kingdom of God.

The truth is, the Church gathered is the way the vast majority of us think of and experience church. We think the church is a group of people gathered in a building for worship and teaching and fellowship. Many of us resonate with Kris's statement because when we think of the Church, we think of our experience of the Church gathered. Part of my mission in this book is to get us to think like Kris (which I think is biblical!) and recognize that we must conceive of the Church and the Kingdom as both gathered *and* distributed.

A more fully orbed biblical understanding of the *ekklesia* means that when believers are operating in culture as the incarnational presence of Jesus, we are bringing the Kingdom of God wherever we go. We are the Church in both expressions, gathered and distributed. When we are gathered and when we are distributed, we are manifesting and extending the Kingdom of God in the world.

I am grateful for the writing and ministry of my friend Ed Silvoso, whose book *Ekklesia* contains a wealth of information about the Kingdom and the *ekklesia*. I highly commend it to you. Here are two particular gleanings regarding the Kingdom that are helpful for our thinking and discerning about the Church:

> Jesus is the One who builds His Church, not us; our assignment is to use the keys of the Kingdom to lock and unlock the Gates of Hades in order for Him to build His Church where those Gates stand. "I will build My church. . . . I will give you the keys of the kingdom of heaven; and whatever you bind on earth shall have been bound in heaven and whatever you loose on earth shall have been loosed in heaven" (Matthew 16:18–19).[2]
>
> Luke 16:16: "The Law and the Prophets were proclaimed until John; since then the gospel of the kingdom of God has been preached, and everyone is forcing his way into it." . . . It is not possible to proclaim the Gospel of the Kingdom using the old paradigms, because the Law and the Prophets announced in the past that something was going to happen in the *future*; whereas the Gospel of the Kingdom focuses on the *present*—the here and now.[3]
>
> Jesus' intention is that the Ekklesia's proclamation of the Gospel of the Kingdom would confront the Gates of Hades now, *in the present*, until those gates collapse so that people, and eventually nations, are transformed.[4]

Let's be clear, then, that the Kingdom of God (and the parallel term, *Kingdom of heaven*) is the Kingdom of the Triune God, and that Jesus is both building and extending His Kingdom here on planet earth. Fascinatingly He chooses to use His followers, gathered in *church* ("Temple courts") and distributed in *culture* ("house to house" and "marketplace") as the incarnational manifestation of His Kingdom—what we know as the *ekklesia*.

We are not only to live "to the praise of his glorious grace" (Ephesians 1:6), but we are to manifest that glory in the everyday reality of our lives. The Church gathered and the Church distributed are the *ekklesia* in action.

Becoming Ambassadors

Romans 14:17 tells us that the Kingdom of God is "righteousness, peace and joy in the Holy Spirit." The presence of God brings all three. But *how* do we see the Kingdom being manifested in its fullness in culture?

I see Matthew 5 as the pinnacle chapter of the Kingdom. The Beatitudes are located there, as is the exhortation for us to be "salt" and "light" in the world:

> "You are the salt of the earth. But if the salt loses its saltiness, how can it be made salty again? It is no longer good for anything, except to be thrown out and trampled underfoot.
>
> "You are the light of the world. A town built on a hill cannot be hidden. Neither do people light a lamp and put it under a bowl. Instead they put it on its stand, and it gives light to everyone in the house. In the same way, let your light shine before others, that they may see your good deeds and glorify your Father in heaven."
>
> Matthew 5:13–16

The exhortation for us to be salt and light provides the framework for Kingdom ambassadorship that is the birthright of every follower of Jesus.

I believe in the Church gathered. I celebrate the Church gathered. I love the Church gathered. It has been my great joy to live in, love and lead the Church gathered. But hear my heart: We have turned the gathering of the Church into an endpoint. Tragically we have missed the Kingdom message of Jesus. **The gathering of the Church is not to be a spectator arena for a Christian entertainment event, but an equipping center for the distribution of the Gospel into the world.**

The Church gathered is to be equipped by the fivefold ministry gifts—apostle, prophet, evangelist, pastor and teacher—so we can be distributed as ambassadors of heaven with the power of the Holy Spirit to reclaim every sphere of society for His glory. We were called to bring heaven to earth as His ambassadors. Rediscovering this truth is an essential piece on our journey to become the distributors of grace that He intends.[5]

In my understanding of the work of the Kingdom, it is my strong belief that our ambassadorship is about pleading with people to be reconciled to God (see 2 Corinthians 5:14–21) and to receive His unmerited favor (grace, or manifested love).

The gathering of the Church is not to be a spectator arena for a Christian entertainment event, but an equipping center for the distribution of the Gospel into the world.

When the Church is gathered, we celebrate and experience the wonder and joy of His grace received. When the Church is distributed, we become ambassadors of reconciliation and distributors of grace to a needy and ministry-starved world. This is the Gospel of Jesus unleashed to bring heaven to earth and see grace distributed. This is New Testament Christianity.

I believe God will bring in an unparalleled harvest as churches contend for the salvation of those in our families, neighborhoods, workplaces and communities who do not know the King of kings.

In Ephesians Paul provides a powerful narrative of who we are and what we have received through faith in Christ:

> Because of his great love for us, God, who is rich in mercy, made us alive with Christ even when we were dead in transgressions—it is by grace you have been saved. And God raised us up with Christ and seated us with him in the heavenly realms in Christ Jesus, in order that in the coming ages he might show the incomparable riches of his grace, expressed in his kindness to us in Christ Jesus. For it is by grace you have been saved, through faith—and this is not from yourselves, it is the gift of God—not by works, so that no one can boast. For we are God's handiwork, created in Christ Jesus to do good works, which God prepared in advance for us to do.
>
> Ephesians 2:4–10

God has not only saved us by grace through faith, but He has "seated us with [Christ] in the heavenly realms," so that His kindness in Jesus may be demonstrated in our world through our walking in the good works that have already been prepared for us. *This* is our assignment and our inheritance. We have a Kingdom ambassadorship, and we traffic in reconciliation and grace! This is the joy that should animate our souls. We have been placed in an atmosphere in which we are equipped for this purpose.

And He has not left us to wonder how. He has even provided specific instructions and guidelines for how He wants us equipped and how He wants grace distributed to our world. That is the subject of the next chapter in our journey.

———————— **BEFORE YOU GO** ————————

When you think of the Church, do you think of a gathering at a specific time and place? Or do you think of the Church distributed with believers in homes and the marketplaces of culture affecting others? When you hear of churches that serve in their communities, do you think of that as the Kingdom of God, or do you put that in another category? Do you have a sense of your own assignment in the Church (*ekklesia*) and in the Kingdom?

5

THE FIVEFOLD MINISTRY AND SPIRITUAL GIFTS

James and Rebecca ended up growing more deeply rooted in their church. The birth of their second child, a girl, caused them even greater depth of connection, while other couples, both young and older, supported them.

James and Rebecca both made strong personal decisions to surrender and yield their lives to Jesus Christ, and they began to understand more deeply and personally what living life in the power of the Holy Spirit meant. On many days when their two kids and their jobs stretched them to the limit, they absolutely knew they could not handle everything in their own natural strength!

Something else started happening about this time: James's parents began to attend church with them—at first occasionally, then monthly, and then most weekends. Even Rebecca's parents started to come on holidays when they were in town.

My hope and prayer is that the Holy Spirit is stirring in you a passion to see the Church corporately, and that you personally experience the presence and power of God in all of life.

As you know, I believe the world stands in desperate need of a second Reformation. That Reformation has not yet been fully birthed because the Body of Christ has participated in only limited (and limiting) worldview understandings, and because we have neglected the clear teaching of Scripture regarding how equipping in the household of faith is to take place.

Because of the need of the hour, many Christians are ready to return to what Jesus intends for His Bride. Covid-19 has been a revealer and accelerator across the planet. Part of what has been revealed is our desperate need to move as the Church family from observation to activation.

Equipping for Ministry

Paul, writing to his dear friends in Ephesus, makes clear that the people of God are to be equipped for ministry through the apostles, prophets, evangelists, pastors and teachers. In our era, sadly, pastors and teachers have been the main operating figures in the leadership hierarchy. Maybe you have thought of church leaders only as pastors or teachers. Maybe you have never met and experienced the leadership of someone with an apostolic, prophetic or evangelistic gifting. Contrast that experience with these words:

> Christ himself gave the apostles, the prophets, the evange-lists, the pastors and teachers, to equip his people for works of service, so that the body of Christ may be built up until we all reach unity in the faith and in the knowledge of the Son

of God and become mature, attaining to the whole measure of the fullness of Christ.

Ephesians 4:11–13

If Christ Himself gave the fivefold ministry gifts "to equip his people for works of service" to build up the Body of Christ so that "we all reach unity in the faith and in the knowledge of the Son of God" in maturity, then why would we neglect these gifts?

I recognize that there has been some measure of controversy over the notion of the fivefold ministry. Many are concerned about the authority of apostles and prophets in the modern era. I will not go further into that discussion here,[1] except to say that we are living in an era when we can find a bridge across several of the streams of the Church (e.g., Reformed, evangelical, charismatic) to walk in the power of the Holy Spirit, so that God's people are equipped and released for ministry and mission in the world. We must operate as the *ekklesia* with what I call a "full employment" policy for each member of the Body. Equipping each person to understand his or her identity, gifting and assignment in the Body of Christ is crucial to helping give birth to the second Reformation.

One helpful way to think about the challenge is to consider whether we understand the mission of the Church as a cruise ship or an aircraft carrier. Are we part of a special club for our own conveniences or a redemptive ambassadorship to reach the world? Many of us have grown so accustomed to church as a place that "meets our needs" and has "programs" to help us and our families that we have lost the biblical mandate for the prevailing nature of the Church.[2] As recent times have demonstrated, we are actually in a battle, not on a scenic vacation tour.[3] Dr. C. Peter Wagner, who as I mentioned in chapter 1 was one of my beloved seminary professors, introduced the aircraft model at a conference many years ago through Pastor Stephen Johnson.[4]

Understanding Our Mission

So what does a Church look like that recognizes she is in a spiritual battle and equips people for their ministry assignments? For me, it is all about the fivefold ministry, equipping the people of God to discover their gifts and ministries.

Equipping and releasing is a central part of bringing heaven to earth. In the fivefold ministry roles (apostles, prophets, evangelists, pastors and teachers), much of the second Reformation will move away from platform and crowd building to discipling and reproducing life and maturity.

Much of our collective experience in first world Christendom, on the other hand, has been about leaders measuring success by the size of our crowds and followings and social media numbers rather than by the generational impact of our equipping ministries.

Jesus had a public ministry for three years; and while He drew large crowds (who went away when His words became too hard to hear), He ultimately left eleven disciples and 120 people in an Upper Room waiting for the Holy Spirit to come and empower them to witness for His glory. I am not sure many of us would invite a modern-day Jesus to address our church leadership conferences, since His three years of public ministry left only 120 frightened followers in that Upper Room!

I hope you will come to believe that discovering our spiritual gifts and unwrapping the packages we have been given is a key part of our spiritual journey in the second Reformation. I have come to believe that discovering and releasing spiritual gifts is essential to the process of spiritual maturity, not some optional experience. You were made to serve the King and His Kingdom, and when you discover how to best serve Him, it will catalyze your spiritual growth. Let me illustrate with a well-known movie plot. In the movie *Cast Away*, Tom Hanks plays a FedEx executive who is flying a plane making last-minute Christmas deliveries. The plane crashes in the Pacific Ocean and Hanks's character floats to an uninhabited island, where he is stranded for five years. During this time he leaves one package salvaged from the wreck unopened, so he can deliver it if he is ever rescued.

After this movie was released, FedEx actually ran a commercial during a subsequent Super Bowl championship game spoofing the film. An actor looking like Hanks has been rescued from the island. He shows up at the address written on the unopened package, to be greeted by the lady of the house. He tells the woman he has been marooned on an island for five years with the package and that he swore to deliver it to her—because he works for FedEx. He hands her the package. She takes it, thanks him and begins to close the door.

Then he asks curiously, "By the way, what's in the package?"

She opens it and says, "Nothing, really, just a satellite phone, GPS locator, fishing rod, water purifier and some seeds."

That is how some of us live! We possess packages that contain exactly what we need, treasures right in front of our noses, and we do not even open them.

Your treasure is your spiritual gift. If you are unaware of it, then it remains an unopened package that contains exactly what you need to find your place in God's plan. I want to help prepare you to be part of the "bringing heaven to earth" movement by discovering your spiritual gifts.

In the next four chapters, I will offer a primer on spiritual gifts, and at the end of chapter 9, I will provide some quick links where you can learn more.

BEFORE YOU GO

Do you know who you are in Christ and what your gifts and ministry assignment are? Have you been equipped by pastors and ministry leaders in church? What was the best form of equipping you ever experienced in a church or conference? Have you ever seen an apostle or prophet working with pastors and teachers in a local church?

6

DISCOVERING YOUR GIFTS

*Just as their spiritual lives seemed to be going well, James
and Rebecca began to grapple in their marriage with the
reality of their differences. The contrasts between their personalities and backgrounds had always been obvious; in fact,
they were part of why they were attracted to each other.
But now, as the two grew spiritually, the differences seemed
to be enlarged. James liked to join groups of people and enjoyed the crowded hallways at church. Rebecca liked people
but enjoyed her times of solitude and reflection more than
the noise of the crowd.*

*In time James and Rebecca would learn to give each other
the space and freedom to be comfortable, but for now those
tension points remained a challenge as they navigated marriage, parenting and spiritual growth.*

Through the years that I have pressed into this revelation of how God intends to bring heaven to earth,
two issues have repeatedly come to the forefront:

First, how do I discover my spiritual gifts? And second, how do I live well in a church family?

I have written this chapter and the three that follow to help you in your journey, praying that the Holy Spirit will use the gifts He has given you to equip you for your unique calling to become a grace ambassador and to help bring heaven to earth. God has fashioned a role for you within His great plan—a crucial place that only you can fill, a special place where you alone fit perfectly. In fact, on a scale of 1 to 10, God created you to be a perfect 10. When you are at your best, everyone around you gets to fulfill his or her special assignment as well (see Ephesians 4:11–16).

When you discover where you fit perfectly, you will also learn how to become the grace ambassador God has called you to be. No longer will days contain a series of disconnected activities that lack meaning or primary focus. Instead, you will live and breathe each moment aware of the call and plan of God for you.

The gifts that God has entrusted to you are not just for you; they are for all of us in the Body of Christ, and for the world around us that does not yet know Jesus as Savior and Lord.

Every Christian has received a specific calling of God to ministry. Do you know your place in God's plan?

The vast majority of us are not employed on a pastoral ministry team in a local church setting. That means our *primary* call to ministry—our place—is within a non-church setting. Our *secondary* call to ministry is within a local church family.

This understanding alone may end up dramatically changing the way you feel about your "everyday" job. You can view your job today—selling cars at the local dealership, processing loans at the bank, leading fitness classes at the gym, or being a stay-at-home mom or dad—through the lens of God's calling for you. This concept will bring freedom to those who view their job as a curse, when in reality it is a calling! (More on this in chapter 10.)

Or it may be that you are one of those who has a primary vocational source of income in a local church family or nonprofit ministry. If so, you and I have a secondary call to the marketplace to influence our world for Christ—as we price cars at the dealership, transact business at the bank, exercise at the gym, and interact in our homes and neighborhoods. It is time we stop thinking that pastors get to serve God full time while those in "regular" jobs can serve God only a few hours a week when we gather at an address for corporate worship. We all serve God full time, every day and everywhere.

Wherever you work and whatever you do, you are serving the Lord of heaven in ministry for His glory (see Colossians 3:17). Everyone in the Body of Christ is serving in ministry. You are a minister!

Launching Spiritual Discovery

So what are the specific gifts with which God has fitted you for service? I want to help you discover the unique place God has for you in His plan, as well as the practical resources He has provided for you in your Kingdom assignment as an ambassador of heaven. Again, remember that when you discover and use your gift, you make me and everyone around you better so we can all use our gifts for His glory.

Galatians 5:13 lays the foundation for our first steps in this spiritual adventure: "You, my brothers and sisters, were called to be free. But do not use your freedom to indulge the flesh; rather, serve one another humbly in love."

Called to be *free*. Don't use *freedom* to indulge the flesh. Use *freedom* to serve one another. What exactly does *freedom* mean?

Let me ask you a question. What if somehow you had complete financial freedom, beginning tomorrow morning? Perhaps you have been dreaming about this your entire life. The moment has arrived, and a huge deposit has been made into your account, and you have no further financial concerns. What will you do with your life at this point? You might imagine taking it easy, lounging around in your pajamas. Maybe around ten o'clock you get dressed to go shopping or play a round of golf. Then perhaps you eat out and see a movie. Finally you have a leisurely supper and watch TV. And when you get up the next morning, you do it all over again. You might think, *If I had total financial freedom, I would have the freedom every single day to do nothing at all!*

Sounds like freedom, right? There are, in fact, studies of people who have done exactly that. They reached retirement after an active, working career, with the goal of doing nothing. But within a few years of their retirement, many of these people felt lost in the freedom of days without structure, and actually died prematurely. They misunderstood the ultimate purpose of freedom: to serve—to do good things, right things—rather than do nothing.

Those, on the other hand, who reach retirement and live vital, healthy, growing, dynamic lives until their last breath are the ones who recognize that our Kingdom assignment is not measured by the hours we clock in at work or the amount of unstructured time we have on the calendar. Kingdom life is about realizing that when we are with our families and colleagues, or when our calendars for the day are filled with structure and responsibility, or when our calendars are free and spontaneous, in every avenue of life we are ambassadors of heaven, and we bring the presence and purposes of God into every conversation, every act of love and every moment of our lives.

Everyday supernatural living is a natural experience of the presence of the Holy Spirit in the relationships and responsibilities of life.

The freedom to do the right thing is a gift of God—and the right thing is to serve God for His glory. In right relationship with Him, you find your place of service in the family of God and bring heaven here on earth.

So what can you do right now to recognize the spiritual gift you have received so you can lean into your assignment from heaven? Put simply, I think the process of spiritual gifts discovery has these three components:

1. Inquire of God

A primary component of spiritual discovery is your own individual search. As you read this book and spend time alone with God as well as in a group, ask Him some hard questions: God, *why did You make me the way I am? Why is it that I have these likes and dislikes? Why am I wired this way?*

2. Inquire of Others

A second component of spiritual discovery is your shared experiences with others. Friends can help you see that a gift you might desire is not the one you were given.

I knew a young man who thought God had called him to be a nationally known country gospel singer. He carried a guitar and wore a cowboy hat everywhere he went. The main problem with his dream was that he did not sing well. He did have a slight twang, but it could not cover up the fact that he sang almost every note flat. Finally some friends said to him, "We love that you love God. We love that you want to serve Him and that you're looking for a way to make an impact with your life. But we don't think being a country gospel singer is God's plan for you." Because they knew him, they were able to redirect him toward goals that better fit his passion and abilities.

Good friends can recognize when we are working outside our giftedness.

Friends can also identify divinely given gifts within us, gifts of which we may be unaware. A friend might say to us, "You know, every time I watch you do this activity, I see God at work." Or, "Every time I hear you talk about that subject, I sense the heartbeat of God in your life."

When we take time for both components—an individual search and a shared discovery—they become powerful mechanisms in our process of spiritual discovery.

3. Identify Your Spiritual DNA

In addition to your individual search and shared experiences with others in this discovery process, consider, too, your "spiritual DNA"—the spiritual hardwiring within you that shapes your perceptions, feelings and behaviors.

There are three dimensions of your spiritual DNA in particular: your passion, gifts and style.

Passion

The first dimension of your spiritual DNA is *passion*—your burden, your call, your sense that "this is why I was created."

For instance, what would you feel if I talked to you about a food distribution program and about hungry people, storage issues and distribution needs? Could you identify with that need because you know what it is like to be hungry or because you have great compassion for people who are hungry? Would you sense what it must be like to have that need met by a generous person? Would your heart beat faster? Would you think, *I can do that. I can take my organizational gifts and be involved there. I have a heart for hungry people.*

Or when you hear about a food program, perhaps you know it is not the passion God has placed in your heart. You might be more attracted to a women's outreach ministry—gathering women to learn about God's love and to care for one another. Or you might be more drawn to children's ministry because you recognize the importance of early childhood development. Maybe it is easy for you to organize things, and you feel excited about going into a church office or library or resource center and transforming chaos into order.

God wants you to serve in areas you feel passionate about. If you currently serve in an area that is not your passion, you may be on the road to burnout. You can be in a church, love God and want to serve Him—yet still become spiritually exhausted. Often burnout happens because people feel obligated and sometimes even guilt-tripped into serving in areas in which they have no giftedness or passion.

We all need to be willing to do things we are not necessarily passionate about. But our primary area of service should be where we feel spiritually energized.

Now, just because we serve in our area of passion does not mean we will not get tired or face obstacles and struggles. Not at all. We may come home at the end of a ministry experience and say, "I'm tired. But God showed up, and I love doing this!"

Gifts

The second dimension of your spiritual DNA is *gifts*. In the next three chapters you will be exposed to about twenty gifts that are mentioned in the Bible. My own view is that this list of gifts is not exhaustive but illustrative. That is, the gifts mentioned in the Bible are not the only spiritual gifts that exist; there may be others as well. But those listed are helpful in presenting categories of gifts so you can more easily find the kinds of gifts you have been given.

God gives you not only passion, then, but specific gifts in order to serve Him in your areas of passion.

Style

The third dimension of your spiritual DNA is personal *style*. This has to do with your unique personality, your distinctive way of thinking, speaking, moving, acting.

Take, for example, Billy Graham. His *passion* was to see people come to know Jesus Christ as Savior and Lord. God gave him the *gift* of evangelism. And his *style* of communicating the Gospel included warm, persuasive preaching in auditoriums and stadiums packed with people. Graham saw amazing things happen over sixty years as he used his winsome style of communicating the good news of Jesus Christ, linked with his passion for lost people and his gift of evangelism. Whenever he spoke to a crowd and gave an invitation for people to give their lives to Jesus, hundreds would stream out of the crowd to receive Christ as Savior.

What about you? You might have a passion to see people come to know Christ, and you might have the spiritual gift of evangelism, yet you might never share Christ in front of a large group of people. But your passion for lost people and your gift for evangelism will play out through your own personal style. You may be a quiet, gentle person whose ministry of evangelism is praying deep, long prayers for family members and friends and coworkers. Your gentle witness in their lives plants seeds that, over time, God nurtures into a harvest. Because you are unique, your manner of serving God is also unique.

Finding Your Perfect Place

Your passion, your gifts and your personal style are linked so that God can bring about His plan and purposes in your life. Psalm 37:4–6 says:

> Take delight in the LORD, and he will give you the desires of your heart. Commit your way to the LORD; trust in him and he will do this: He will make your righteous reward shine like the dawn, your vindication like the noonday sun.

Take time right now to write two words on a piece of paper. First write the word *delight;* then draw a line connecting it with the second word, *desires.* Psalm 37:4 says, "Take delight in the LORD, and he will give you the desires of your heart."

I used to read that verse as saying, "If I delight myself in God, I can get anything I want." Over time, as I studied the words, I have come to believe that it is absolutely true—if I delight myself in God, He will give me the desires of my heart. But let me drill a bit further into these words. If I delight myself in God, He will make it so that the desires of my heart are completely fulfilled. If I learn to delight myself in Him, I will want what God wants for my life. My highest aspiration will be not for my personal success, but to fit successfully into God's plan.

Now I ask you to write two other words. Write the word *commit*; then draw a line connecting it to the word *trust*. Your commitment to spiritual growth is essential to fully experiencing God's plan for your life.

I recognize that you are likely reading this book on your own, and I am grateful for that. Ideally, however, I would love for you to join others who know and love you, so they can help you discover and affirm your spiritual gifts. Perhaps you can be the one who convenes a small group for a few weeks to pray and read through these materials and help each other discover your heaven-given gifts and assignments.

During the process of discovering your spiritual gifts, I pray that you will encounter God and that God will reveal to you why He made you the way He has. I pray that you encounter relationships with others so they can confirm the gifts God has given you, or help you to reorient if you are on the wrong path.

Either way, may God use all these experiences to help you determine your perfect place in His plan. God wants to create a radical experience in the soil of your soul so you can live celebrating His glory and honor. The discovery process is all about identifying God's plans for you in His family, and I believe the results will revolutionize your world.

BEFORE YOU GO

Do you have background understanding on the subject of spiritual gifts or is this new to you? If you have background, do you feel confident in knowing how you are particularly gifted? Have you ever wondered if your gifts could change through the years? Think about a time when someone affirmed what he or she believed was your special gift or assignment in the family. Do you think other people see you more clearly than you see yourself, or do you believe you see yourself the most clearly?

7

YOU FIT INTO THE FAMILY

The small group had become a staple of James's and Rebecca's weekly life. The small group (it was called a "life group" in their church) met James's quest for energy and interaction, while Rebecca loved the depth and intimacy of the relationships they experienced.

James and Rebecca grew to trust the members of their small group and value them as extended family members. In the midst of their changing and challenging world (not to mention the occasional sleep-deprived nights with their two little ones), the small group was a safe place to be.

Spiritual growth happens in community. I am not saying you cannot have a spiritual experience alone. On the contrary, Scripture urges people as they are growing spiritually to find moments of solitude when they can "be still, and know that I am God" (Psalm 46:10). However, God also places His children in communities of faith where we can be supported and safeguarded as we discover our gifts. His plan for your life requires that you be in loving relationships with others.

In John 13, when Jesus was in the Upper Room with His disciples before His betrayal and crucifixion, we see Him at the end of His earthly ministry.

When some people get to the end of their time on earth, they try to set things in order, making sure everything is taken care of, that their families will be well attended to and that their last wishes and instructions are known. That is what Jesus was doing. Knowing His time was short and that He would soon leave this earth, Jesus spoke these important words:

> "A new command I give you: Love one another. As I have loved you, so you must love one another. By this everyone will know that you are my disciples, if you love one another."

> John 13:34–35

Jesus was commanding His disciples—then and now—to be in loving relationships with one another, to have a circle of people with whom they could meaningfully relate.

Contrast this example from the life of Jesus with what some people do when visiting churches. The first step they take is to enjoy the anonymity. This is a purposeful choice. At first they do not want to feel pressured to tell anyone their life story. They do not have to be vulnerable or transparent. They want to take a step but not a plunge. Some people do that for weeks. Sadly, some do it for years unending.

But the place of anonymity is not the place of ultimate spiritual health. We must decide to be in meaningful relationship with others.

We Are Unique

It is a common parenting goal to raise children who are self-reliant and independent. And it is considered the pinnacle of success for someone to claim to be a "self-made" man or woman. I suggest, however, that everyone stands on the shoulders of those who have gone before.

I do not know all that you have been through, but the freedom you have to declare yourself a self-made man or woman is possible because people before you paid the price of freedom with their blood. At the very minimum, even if you have accomplished a lot because of your efforts, remember that others made it possible for you to be free to become who you are. All of us have people who have invested in our lives, even if that investment was in the systems or governments that shape the culture in which we live.

If you are a follower of Christ, or if you are searching for God, remember that you stand on the shoulders of others who have gone before you.

A critical aspect to being in loving relationships with others involves knowing this: *You were made special order.* That is a powerful fact to understand. Some people almost think God must have a widget factory in heaven that makes people in only four or five basic varieties. But the Bible teaches that you are a unique human being. No one else on the planet is like you. Let's look at a well-known Bible passage:

> You created my inmost being; you knit me together in my mother's womb. I praise you because I am fearfully and wonderfully made; your works are wonderful, I know that full well. My frame was not hidden from you when I was made in the secret place, when I was woven together in the depths

of the earth. Your eyes saw my unformed body; all the days ordained for me were written in your book before one of them came to be.

Psalm 139:13–16

Our task as parents and grandparents is to identify and call forth—to understand and draw out—the uniqueness God created in our children. Each child has distinctive characteristics that parents can help develop. Some children, even by age four or five, begin demonstrating the traits of an attorney; they have the ability to argue their case brilliantly. Other children reveal a teaching gene and instruct their parents on how things should be. Still other children have an engineering gene and start taking things apart because they are fascinated by how things work.

Each one of us is a unique creation of God and precious in his sight.

Healthy Cautions for Loving Families

Just as God puts children in families, so God also puts believers in church families that provide home groups, ministries, classes and other ways for people to connect in loving relationships. That does not mean you should be best friends with fifty people, or even fifteen. But there should be a few people who know and love you well enough to speak life and hope to you, as well as challenge you when you are doing less than your best.

In light of our need for close, trusted friends, I would like to share three cautions based on more than forty years of pastoral experience and a lifetime spent in church families.

Caution: Projection

The first caution is the temptation of *projection*—when others tell us what they see in us because it is really what they see in themselves. I suspect you have experienced situations—I know I have—when someone told you what he or she believed was God's plan for your life, when that plan sure sounded like that person's own opinion about what your life should be about, or even what that person's own life should be about.

We pray about each of these circumstances when someone talks with us, but we need to discern whether it is the Holy Spirit speaking to us or that person projecting his or her own perceptions onto us.

When the prophet Isaiah was in the Temple, he saw a vision of the Lord seated on His throne, and he heard the voice of God saying, "Whom shall I send? And who will go for us?" (Isaiah 6:8). Did Isaiah respond to God, saying, "Here I am, Lord, send *him*"? No, of course not. He actually said, "Here am I. Send me!" (verse 8).

So when you invite people into your life, be discerning about what they say to you. We are all guilty of projection from time to time.

Caution: Elevation

A second caution relates to the issue of *elevation*. Elevation occurs when others puff you up because of your gifting. That is, they overemphasize the effects of your gifts. They may even start to believe that you are so gifted by God that you do not have ordinary struggles.

While it is helpful to have people speak life and affirmation into your service for God, be cautious not to forget that everything you are and everything you have, you received by grace, not by merit.

Gifts are not things to boast about. Be careful of elevating yourself or letting others do it for you.

Caution: Rejection

The third caution is the flipside to elevation, *rejection*. Rejection takes place when people see no good in you. Every time they speak to you, they speak toxins to your soul. They stick pinpricks into the balloons of your life. These are negative, critical people and we must recognize them as such and not allow them access to the interior parts of our souls.

Just as the people who elevate you can cause you to think wrongly (by believing you are uncommonly good), so people who reject you can also cause you to think wrongly (by believing you are a failure). Another way to say this is that *hurt people hurt people*. People who are themselves hurting tend to wound others as a way of life. Be careful whom you allow access to your soul and eliminate both elevation and rejection.

God has a unique design for your life and wants your relationships with others to be characterized by love—the kind of love Paul described in 1 Corinthians 13:1–8:

> If I speak in the tongues of men or of angels, but do not have love, I am only a resounding gong or a clanging cymbal. If I have the gift of prophecy and can fathom all mysteries and all knowledge, and if I have a faith that can move mountains, but do not have love, I am nothing. If I give all I possess to the poor and give over my body to hardship that I may boast, but do not have love, I gain nothing.
>
> Love is patient, love is kind. It does not envy, it does not boast, it is not proud. It does not dishonor others, it is not self-seeking, it is not easily angered, it keeps no record of wrongs. Love does not delight in evil but rejoices with the

truth. It always protects, always trusts, always hopes, always perseveres. Love never fails.

What a powerful description of the nature of loving relationships that God calls us to! The standard for love is high; the reality we experience is often low. But this passage does not describe natural human love. It is not about your love as a husband or wife, mother or father, grandma or grandpa, aunt or uncle, or friend. This passage is about the nature of God's love. To the extent that you allow God's love to flow through you to other people, you will be able to experience the 1 Corinthians 13 kind of love in your life and in the ministry of your gifts.

Find and help create that kind of family so you can be part of bringing heaven to earth as an ambassador of grace in your everyday life.

BEFORE YOU GO

Spiritual growth happens in community. Do you have two or three people who know all about you and yet still care about you? Have you been able to receive love and encouragement from someone in your past? When you think of gratitude for your freedom to become who God made you to be, is there a person or moment in history that you think about? Have you been able to contribute to someone else's life to give that person opportunity?

8

THE FOUNDATION OF SPIRITUAL GIFTS

James and Rebecca were starting to feel that Jesus was the center of their lives, and their church family was core to the experience. Recently the church had begun to teach a class on spiritual gifts, and James and Rebecca were able to juggle the class along with their small group, work and parenting responsibilities.

Rebecca discovered that she had a gift for teaching, which surprised even herself. She began serving periodically with children and women a bit younger than she was. James was equally surprised to discover his administrative gifts and a real passion for helping others.

James and Rebecca were tired at times, but the moments when they served with their newly discovered gifts were some of the best in their lives.

Many years ago, as a church planter in Nevada when our first church building was being built, I learned something about foundations. Meeting in temporary facilities, we wanted desperately to get into our permanent building. But it seemed to take months for the construction crew to finish laying the foundation. Really it was only weeks, but it seemed longer, as the earth-moving equipment drove back and forth and back and forth, leveling the land and compacting the soil. I grew extremely frustrated at the pace, wondering why it was taking so long.

But one day the foreman called and said, "We're pouring the concrete pad for the foundation tomorrow. We'll start pouring at three in the morning."

I was shocked by the early hour, but headed to the site the next morning, coffee and doughnuts in hand, to videotape the work. By 8:30 a.m. they had finished pouring the huge concrete slab for the foundation. Then they smoothed it. Even then they were not quite finished. When the slab appeared smooth, they shot a laser beam across the foundation from different angles, making sure, carefully and precisely, that it was perfectly level.

At first I did not understand why laying the foundation took so much time. It seemed better to me to start constructing the building itself so people could see something happening and get excited. (The people had to be glad I was the pastor and not the general contractor!) Then, a few weeks after the slab was poured, cranes lifted the first huge concrete panels, set them vertically and placed them onto the foundation pad. When the side panels of concrete were up, workers connected them with roof trusses and began building the roof structure above it all.

As the building took shape, I realized just how much weight was resting on the soil and foundation. At that moment I was grateful for the weeks of work spent ensuring that the building was stable and exactly vertical and true.

This understanding of the importance of building a foundation has shaped the rest of my life as I think about how important foundations are for building structures that last and that can withstand the storms of the surrounding environment.

In this chapter we will lay a general foundation for understanding spiritual gifts. God has equipped His family with spiritual gifts. Discovering yours will equip you to fulfill God's purpose for your life. The next chapter will cultivate a deeper understanding of specific gifts and give you some resources to identify and begin to move forward in your use of the gifts.

If we do not lay a proper foundation, the entire structure may be in danger. So we start in this chapter with laying that solid foundation on the topic of spiritual gifts. I hope and pray that you will discover the special gifts and capacities God has placed within you as a grace ambassador.

I know how excited we can be when we open up gifts on special occasions. I believe that when you discover your gifts, you will be even more excited to become an ambassador of heaven to earth with your special, God-given tools.

1 Corinthians 12

When trying to understand a topic, it is sometimes good to review the Bible from cover to cover to see what it says about that topic.

At other times we can go to a particular section of Scripture to find a key teaching on it. If we want to know about the tenderness of God, for instance, we might go to Psalm 23, the Shepherd's Psalm, describing the tenderness with which God loves us, as a shepherd cares for his sheep. If we want to know about the love of God and the character and nature of that love, we might go to 1 Corinthians 13, the love chapter, because it contains a beautiful, poetic, powerful description of love.

Several passages in the New Testament talk about spiritual gifts. The key passage is found in 1 Corinthians 12.

In the first verse of this chapter, Paul tells us, "Now about the gifts of the Spirit, brothers and sisters, I do not want you to be uninformed." God wants to draw our attention to this topic. If we love Jesus and want to fulfill God's purpose in our lives, we need to pay attention to this text about spiritual gifts, which are foundational to our spiritual lives and not simply optional equipment for the journey.

In verses 4–6 we read,

> There are different kinds of gifts, but the same Spirit distributes them. There are different kinds of service, but the same Lord. There are different kinds of working, but in all of them and in everyone it is the same God at work.

Let's examine what these verses mean.

It's All about the Giver

Verse 4 says, "There are different kinds of gifts, but the same Spirit." There is only one Spirit, and He distributes spiritual gifts to believers. Verse 5 says, "There are different kinds of service, but the same Lord." *Service* refers to the ministries in which the gifts are used. And verse 6 tells us, "There are different kinds of working"—that is, effects or results—"but the same God at work." In other words, using a gift in a ministry will have an impact, but there is only one Spirit, or one God, who works all these things together.

If there are different gifts but one Spirit, different ministries but one Lord, and different effects but only one God, then what does the working of spiritual gifts and the impact of all that have to do with me—with my worth or value? *Absolutely nothing!* If, when focusing on spiritual gifts, we find ourselves looking at the individual who is the recipient of the gift, or if we find ourselves looking at the impact or outworking of the gift, instead of looking at the God who gave the gift, then we are getting a distorted view of the purpose and meaning of the gift.

The reality is that the gifts, ministries and results are all about the Father, the Son and the Holy Spirit, not about us. If we do not get that straight, we will be distorted in our experience and use of the gifts. We will get it all confused if we focus on the effect of the gift or on the person who has the gift—and we will lose our focus on God.

Spiritual gifts are an arena in which each member of the Triune God (Father, Son, Holy Spirit) is in relationship with us and gifting us with His presence, blessing and assignment.

Let me give a couple of illustrations. Let's say that you think you have the gift of exhortation—the gift of building up or challenging people to grow deeper in their relationship with God. Let's say you want to exercise that gift in singing, because God also gave you a powerful voice. So you study, prepare and plan. Your dream is to use your gift in a stadium so you can minister as a solo artist to thousands of people. Instead of that opportunity, however, you are asked to lead worship in a small group of twelve people, six of whom sing off key. If you do not understand gifts and ministries and effects, you might get angry about that "lesser" opportunity.

Or let's say your gift is teaching. Your dream is to teach in a small group setting, so you prepare for that ministry. Then the opportunity arrives. But instead of a small group of twelve or so, only two people show up, and they can barely stay awake.

Only when we understand that gifts and ministries and effects are about God will we be at peace with our assignment from Him. Spiritual gifts come from God. Ministry opportunities are assigned by God. And the effects are ultimately up to God. We can be open to an assignment only when we are at peace with the fact that it is God who distributes the gift, God who assigns the ministry and God who decides the outworking of it all. Serving God is about God. It is not about us.

Different Seasons

An experience from my own life might be a window for us all. Before planting our church in Carson Valley, Nevada, I was serving at the denominational level, meeting with some ministry leaders whose teaching effectiveness had clearly diminished and who had reached the end of their public ministry lives. This made me think about my own life and ministry.

We all need to be clear about what season of life we are in and when it would be best for us to move into other realms of service. Personally, I have prayed that I can serve faithfully in specific roles and also recognize when it is time for me to move into other ministry assignments. My prayer is that I will have the spiritual maturity to serve in a different capacity for the sake of the Kingdom of God when my current assignment is over and I enter a different season of my life.

Given to Each, Used for All

First Corinthians 12:7 gives another interesting foundational truth about spiritual gifts: "To each one the manifestation of the Spirit is given for the common good." This tells us that every Christ-follower has at least one spiritual gift. This is a truth worth celebrating!

In our home, Pam and I have had the experience of inviting people over to celebrate Christmas and discovering, to our horror, that somebody came at the last minute for whom we did not have a gift. That is an awkward situation, to say the least! In our house, that experience throws us into a panic, and Pam wonderfully finds and wraps an appropriate gift immediately so that person is not left out of the gift exchange.

Spiritual life is different. It is not a party where somebody shows up and leaves without a gift. If you are a Christ-follower, you have been invited to the table and a gift is prepared for you.

I am convinced, however, that many of us go through the journey of life with wrapped gifts that remain unopened (like the Tom Hanks character I described earlier). Romans 12:4–5 says,

> Just as each of us has one body with many members, and these members do not all have the same function, so in Christ we, though many, form one body, and each member belongs to all the others.

The truth is, God has a place for you in His plan, and this place is matched with your spiritual gift. You must open and understand the gift He has given you and put it into play.

Using Your Gift Well

Some years ago I came across seven observations about spiritual gifts made by A. T. Pierson,[1] Presbyterian pastor and missiologist in the late nineteenth century. I have found these seven points most helpful, and share them with you here in slightly updated language, with a few comments following each one.

1. *Every believer has at least one gift, so everyone should be encouraged.* If you are a Christ-follower, you should be encouraged because you were invited to the party and God has a gift for you.

2. *No one has all the gifts, so everyone should be humble.* Jesus was the only One to walk the face of the earth perfectly equipped to do every job description in the Kingdom. Since you and I do not have all the gifts, we need the gifts of others to complement our own. This realization helps keep us humble.

3. *All the gifts are for Christ's work, so all work should be harmonious.* If we focus only on the project at hand, or on each other, or on our conflicts, we will lose the harmony we should be enjoying. Since our gifts are for the work of Jesus, keeping our eyes on Him will help build unity where disunity would be natural. We must remember that we are all working for the same Boss.

4. *All gifts are to be used for Christ's glory, so everyone should be content.* This is challenging. Occasionally we see Christians who, because of their spiritual gifts, have an attitude of superiority over other Christians. They elevate themselves, thinking their gifts are more important than those of others. We talked in the last chapter about not elevating ourselves or letting others do it for us. How foolish to use our gifts as an excuse for pride! We have nothing that we did not receive by grace and for the glory of God.

5. *All gifts are to build up the Body of Christ, so all are needed and helpful.* We need to be careful how we use our gifts. We should never use them in ways that bring destruction or defeat or discouragement. We should take care to build up one another in Christ so that the Body matures.

6. *All gifts are for spiritual health, so all are necessary.* God designed the gifts and distributes them as He sees fit. We need all the spiritual gifts since all work together for the health of the spiritual community.

7. *All gifts require God's Spirit at work, so we should keep in close touch with Him.* If we want to use the gifts God has entrusted to the Church in ways that give Him glory and honor, and that fulfill His purpose for us and for the Church in the world, we must walk in the light of God's Word and in the power and rhythm of the indwelling Holy Spirit.

Let me tell you a mistake I made earlier in my Christian life. When I watched somebody who had an obvious gift of God, I would jump to the wrong conclusion. I would see the ministry that person had been assigned, and the obvious effect of that gift on others, and assume that he or she was a spiritually mature person. This was a natural reaction, but not at all true in the supernatural realm.

I want to be clear on this point: *It is possible for a person to have a spiritual gift, to be assigned to a ministry, and for a time see powerful effects, and yet be self-centered, ambitious for personal advantage and glory, and driven by the flesh rather than by the Spirit.* When immature people have a positive impact, that is a testimony to the grace and power of God to use flawed and failing vessels for His glory and honor.

Spiritual gifts and ministries and effects have nothing to do with spiritual maturity. They have to do with how God has chosen to work in the world. Sometimes God entrusts great gifts to immature people, giving them opportunities to do ministry and produce wonderful effects. Tragically the results can also be disastrous. If we do not depend on God throughout the process of doing ministry, we, too, will eventually go off into the ditch, taking a host of people with us.

The televangelist scandals in the mid-1980s were a formative influence in my life. I observed a number of people whom God had clearly entrusted with powerful gifts. He gave them huge ministry opportunities that brought about tremendous results. Some of those leaders, however, started thinking it was all about their personal power and glory, not about God's.

We must be careful to avoid the pride that leads to destruction. The gifts of God are powerful, and we must exercise meekness and caution, using them exclusively to glorify God, not ourselves.

BEFORE YOU GO

Do you feel that you understand spiritual gifts? Have you had experiences in which the focus seemed to be on the person with the gift or on the experience of the gift rather than on God? God has distributed His gifts across His family and given us different ministries and effects. Can you articulate what you think is your primary way to follow God and serve Him at this time in your life?

9

SPIRITUAL GIFTS FOR THE
SECOND REFORMATION

James and Rebecca felt as if their lives of serving and min-
istry were paralleling the lives of their kids. Just as they had
witnessed the birth, development, crawling, walking and
talking of their two babies—now children—they felt the
same about the use of their spiritual gifts. Learning that
they had gifts and that they could use them to serve God
and others was an exciting journey.

It was frustrating when they made mistakes, discovered
what they were not good at, and experienced the learning curve
in the use of their gifts. But, thankfully, their church family
made the use of spiritual gifts to be an adventure; and James
and Rebecca felt acceptance rather than condemnation, and
the freedom to fail rather than the expectation of perfection.

In the previous chapter, I laid a solid foundation for understanding spiritual gifts. In this chapter I want to give you
a second layer of teaching about spiritual gifts so you can

be personally equipped for your role in the second Reformation, the "bringing heaven to earth" movement, and so you can share with others as well.

Let's look at five passages in the New Testament that talk about spiritual gifts.

First, 1 Corinthians 12:7–11:

> Now to each one [that means every person who is a Christ-follower] the manifestation of the Spirit is given for the common good. To one there is given through the Spirit a message of wisdom, to another a message of knowledge by means of the same Spirit, to another faith by the same Spirit, to another gifts of healing by that one Spirit, to another miraculous powers, to another prophecy, to another distinguishing between spirits, to another speaking in different kinds of tongues, and to still another the interpretation of tongues. All these are the work of one and the same Spirit, and he distributes them to each one, just as he determines.

A second key passage is found later in the same chapter:

> God has placed in the Church first of all apostles, second prophets, third teachers, then miracles, then gifts of healing, of helping, of guidance and of different kinds of tongues. Are all apostles? Are all prophets? Are all teachers? Do all work miracles? Do all have gifts of healing? Do all speak in tongues? Do all interpret? Now eagerly desire the greater gifts.
>
> verses 28–31

This part of the chapter talks about apostles, prophets, evangelists, pastors and teachers. Some believe these are not spiritual gifts, but rather offices in the Church. Reasonable Christians can disagree on this point. My position is that while these are indeed offices in the Church, they also require

98

specific gifts. In other words, the office of apostle requires the gift of apostleship; the office of teacher requires the gift of teaching; and so on. It makes sense that they are not solely offices, but also gifts that equip those who hold those offices.

Let me also say that even when someone does not have the gift of evangelism, the Holy Spirit can evangelize through that person. Even if a person does not have the gift of healing, the Holy Spirit can heal through that person. Even though each gift is a special supernatural endowment, we all get to "do the stuff" (as John Wimber, founder of the Vineyard movement, used to say about ministry). The Holy Spirit distributes the gift as He wills.

Paul's questions at the end of the second passage are rhetorical, and each expects a negative answer: No, not everyone works miracles, not everyone has gifts of leadership, not everyone has gifts of mercy, not everyone speaks in tongues. And Paul exhorts his readers to "eagerly desire the greater gifts."

Romans 12:6–8 is a third important passage on the topic of spiritual gifts. Paul writes:

> We have different gifts, according to the grace given to each of us. If your gift is prophesying, then prophesy in accordance with your faith; if it is serving, then serve; if it is teaching, then teach; if it is to encourage, then give encouragement; if it is giving, then give generously; if it is to lead, do it diligently; if it is to show mercy, do it cheerfully.

There are two other passages we will review. Ephesians 4:11 says, "Christ himself gave the apostles, the prophets, the evangelists, the pastors and teachers. . . ." And 1 Peter 4:9–10 says, "Offer hospitality to one another without grumbling. Each of you should use whatever gift you have received to serve others."

Wait a minute—offer hospitality? What does that have to do with spiritual gifts? Verse 9 says, "Offer hospitality," and verse 10 says, "Use whatever gift you have." In the Greek, verses 9 and 10 form one sentence, so most people connect them and say that hospitality is actually a gifting from God. Some people have a supernatural ability to encourage others by making them feel warmly welcomed.

Continuing in 1 Peter 4:

> Each of you should use whatever gift you have received to serve others, as faithful stewards of God's grace in its various forms. If anyone speaks, they should do so as one who speaks the very words of God. If anyone serves, they should do so with the strength God provides, so that in all things God may be praised through Jesus Christ. To him be the glory and the power for ever and ever. Amen.
>
> verses 10–11

When we go through those six passages and list the different gifts, eliminating duplicates, we have somewhere between 19 and 21 spiritual gifts. I think these listings are illustrative, however, rather than exhaustive. That is, they represent a general listing of gifts, which does not limit God's creativity in gifting every believer uniquely for some particular service in the Body of Christ.

In my pastoral teaching, I have grouped the New Testament gifts into four ministry categories as a way of organizing them and helping us understand something of their functions. The categories I use are these: *ministry growth gifts*, *ministry support gifts*, *ministry protection gifts* and *ministry sign gifts*.

Let's look at each category in more detail.

1. Ministry Growth Gifts

The first category we will consider, ministry growth gifts, refers to gifts useful in establishing new churches and in developing and growing ministries.

Apostleship

The first ministry growth gift is apostleship—the ability to extend God's ministry into unreached areas and to influence movements of people. Some missionaries use the apostolic gift as they travel into unreached territories. God calls them into areas where the good news of Jesus has never been preached. (The word *apostle* means "one sent forth.") Then there are people with the apostolic gift who have influence and authority over movements of people.

In the book of Acts, for example, we see the apostles—who experienced the living Christ face to face—exercising unique leadership in the early Church. Not only in the first century, but today, the gift of apostleship—extending the Gospel to unreached areas and influencing entire movements—is still very real and very important to the mission of the Church.

Prophecy

The second ministry growth gift is prophecy—declaring the Word of God with power. Some people think that prophets only foretold future events. Not at all. Most of the time the biblical prophets were not "foretelling" the future, but "forthtelling" the truth of God to the nation of Israel. They were speaking words God gave them to inform Israel of the consequences of obeying and disobeying His laws, spelled out in their covenant with Him.

In the New Testament, prophecy is listed as one of the greater gifts (see 1 Corinthians 14:1).

101

Although I do not have this gift, there have been many times when, in communicating God's Word, I could sense the Spirit of God taking over. The words that came out of my mouth, and the ways in which God's Spirit was penetrating people's hearts, caused me to realize that my anointed preparation and careful deliberation had nothing to do with the effects. The Spirit of God was working in a prophetic, forthtelling manner to proclaim the words of God with power to change people's hearts.

Pastoring

The third ministry growth gift is pastoring—shepherding other believers to spiritual maturity. People may never serve in the office of pastor, yet still have a pastoring or shepherding gift, a call to be a spiritual mentor for others. These people have a gifting to help others grow in their faith from infancy to maturity. Discipleship, or helping people grow to spiritual maturity, is essential for spiritual health, both individually and corporately.

Teaching

The fourth ministry growth gift is teaching—communicating God's Word effectively to believers and unbelievers alike.

John R. W. Stott, theologian, pastor and much-loved Bible teacher, referred to a practice of theologian Karl Barth, saying that the goal of the communicator, the teacher of God's Word, is to practice "double listening"—taking the newspaper in one hand, the Bible in the other and building a bridge between the two, so the timeless truth of God's Word connects with the reality of today's news.[1]

A person with a teaching gift can tell us what God's Word says and how it relates to our daily lives.

Evangelism

The fifth ministry growth gift is evangelism—sharing the Gospel to reach people for Christ.

My dad had the gift of evangelism. He enjoyed witnessing for Jesus in restaurants, at gas stations and especially on airplanes—because, he said, where are people going to go? It was the ultimate captive audience. We kids were often embarrassed about Dad's aggressive sharing during those times.

Over the last ten years of his life, he hung out at two local doughnut shops with his World War II buddies. At his funeral service, about fifteen people talked about the impact Dad had in sharing his faith at those doughnut shops. Some were believers in Christ; others had not yet committed their lives to Him. But out of respect for the impact he had on them, they came to his memorial service. His evangelism talks at the doughnut shops, I believe, resulted in expanding not only some waistlines but the Kingdom of heaven as well.

Leadership

The sixth ministry growth gift is leadership—the God-given ability to envision the future and equip people to get there. In the Church there are people with the ability to see the future, seize it and bring it into the present. If you have been around people with a leadership gift, you have no doubt heard them describe the future. Theirs is not the fanciful description of some ungrounded dreamer, but a vision from God about where to go.

This and the other five ministry growth gifts equip and enable the Body of Christ to go where God is leading, fulfilling His vision for His Church.

2. Ministry Support Gifts

Those with ministry support gifts serve in support roles for the Body of Christ.

Administration

The gift of administration includes mobilizing and galvanizing God's people to accomplish His purposes.

I used to think the gift of administration was the ability to move paper from one side of the desk to another. What I have discovered over time is that the gift of administration is vital, especially for a large church or ministry. Many larger churches, for example, have thriving children's ministries caring for hundreds of young people in the faith. The classes are typically supplied with all the necessary resources for teaching, crafts, snacks and music. You can be assured that some administratively gifted people in the children's ministry are running things behind the scenes, making sure the in-class ministry folks have whatever they need to touch a child's heart.

Helps

The gift of helps is serving in a capacity to ensure that ministry happens wherever, whenever. I love people with the gift of helps because they are willing to do whatever it takes to help out and they do not care who gets the credit.

When we were starting our church in Nevada, I prayed first that God would send people with the gift of giving. I will not lie—we really needed generous givers in those days! But I also prayed for people with the gift of helps.

We needed a lot of help. Every single week we had to set up and tear down in temporary locations. We used carts to move things in and out, starting at 6:30 on Sunday mornings.

You have to be a person with the gift of helps to be willing to do all that behind-the-scenes work! But sure enough, every week people with this gift set up, tore down, served doughnuts, handed out programs, wiped noses in children's classes and so much more.

People gifted with helps are willing to do whatever it takes to abundantly serve those who come.

Exhortation

Believers equipped with the gift of exhortation encourage and admonish others toward spiritual maturity. In the New Testament the Pauline epistles are full of exhortation and encouragement. When we read about Paul's heartbeat for the churches he had planted, we recognize this gift in the life of Paul himself.

When we speak to one another in love, we build each other up in our faith. Those with the gift of exhortation watch God use them to strengthen other believers (see Ephesians 4:25–32).

Giving

The gift of giving is the supernatural capacity (and accompanying joy) to give generously in order to see the Body of Christ reach the world. People with the gift of giving are overjoyed that they can give time, use their talents, and give of the treasure God entrusts to them. Let me tell you two quick examples.

My younger brother, Gene, has the gift of giving. He is a behind-the-scenes, let-me-at-it, let-me-do-this kind of guy. He also has the gift of faith, so he is always dreaming bigger than most of us are able to. Gene is a visionary who is willing to give time, talent and treasure to see God's future happen.

R. G. LeTourneau is another example. For years he believed God had called him to be a missionary or pastor. But the more he pursued it, the more it became clear that he was not supposed to be in "vocational ministry"—earning his living from working for a church or Christian organization. God had given him extraordinary ability as an engineer, and in the first half of the twentieth century, he became one of the primary developers of earth-moving equipment. Later, as a very wealthy man, LeTourneau made the Kingdom decision for himself and his company to "reverse tithe"—live on 10 percent of his income and give away 90 percent.

LeTourneau never became the preacher he wanted to be, although he maintained Christian speaking engagements around the world. But God combined his gift of giving with amazing engineering skills to produce substantive resources to fund the Kingdom of God for effective ministry.

Mercy

The gift of mercy is the capacity to care, to come alongside, to empathize and to be Jesus-with-skin-on to those in need. People with this gift want to bring relief to immediate needs. They feel compassion toward those in the hospital and those struggling with physical, financial, emotional or spiritual problems. People with the gift of mercy have deep empathy that makes them effective in relating God's love to those who are hurting.

Hospitality

The gift of hospitality is the ability to communicate a warm welcome that enriches people and makes them feel comfortable in unfamiliar surroundings. People with this gift create an environment in which others feel valued and cared for, especially regarding fellowship, food, lodging. People with the gift of hospitality make friends easily and seek ways to connect with others in meaningful relationships.

3. Ministry Protection Gifts

Ministry protection gifts are those that challenge and guard the flock. These gifts help keep the Body of Christ a safe place where people can grow. If a local body of believers lacks the gifts of knowledge, wisdom, faith and discernment, then evil, untruth and deception can get in and wreak havoc.

Knowledge and Wisdom

The gifts of knowledge and wisdom are companion gifts.

Believers with the gift of knowledge have exceptional insight into the truths of God's Word or into the circumstances of people's lives. People with this gift are able to systematize and summarize Scripture to explain it to others, and they are often able to reveal something to another person that only the Holy Spirit could have given them, thus blessing and increasing faith in that other person.

The gift of wisdom is the ability to use God's Word to transform daily life into spiritual service. People with this gift can sort through conflict and confusion and offer direction, enabling themselves or other people to make godly decisions. They have the insight to understand how knowledge can best be applied to specific situations.

Faith

The gift of faith is the ability to see God's invisible plan and believe it, despite the current visible reality. It takes no faith to believe that a snowball rolling downhill will keep going. But it takes faith to believe that the snowball you are currently pushing uphill will finally make it over the hilltop.

Those with the gift of faith have an unwavering confidence in God's power to bring unity out of hostility, peace out of storms and good out of evil.

Discernment

The gift of discernment is the ability to determine whether something or someone is of God, of the flesh (human nature) or of the adversary, the evil one. The gift of discernment is the ability to distinguish truth from error and sincerity from hypocrisy. Those with discernment can sense the presence of evil.

Do you remember the Bible teaching that Satan "masquerades as an angel of light" (2 Corinthians 11:14)? In this way the enemy is able to twist things, confuse issues and deceive people. People with the gift of discernment can listen to something and know whether it is from God or not.

4. Ministry Sign Gifts

The last category of gifts is ministry sign gifts. Four gifts make up this category: healing, miracles, tongues and interpretation of tongues.

These gifts concern evangelism and obedience, and are often used as God's vehicle to extend His work into an unreached area. These gifts are for today. And they can be controversial.

Ministry sign gifts have sometimes been experienced in settings in which the atmosphere seemed chaotic—perhaps involving singing and dancing and what seemed like "irrational exuberance." If you are a new Christian or not yet a Christian, these may be some of the gifts that made you feel uncomfortable. And while God is a God of order and not chaos (see 1 Corinthians 14:33), I believe He wants us to understand and experience these gifts to the Church, His Body.

If what I have just said troubles you in any way, please read 1 Corinthians 14 for more insight on this issue.

The church of Corinth had severe spiritual problems. They exercised all the gifts we have mentioned, but they abused them by having a "magic party" every weekend. Their church meetings were chaotic, and nobody was being drawn closer to God. They promoted people with showy gifts, instead of promoting unity and love. In 1 Corinthians 14, Paul corrected this behavior with a strong word of exhortation. (Okay, call it what it was—a rebuke!)

The enemy of our souls is always trying to corrupt what the Father gives us for our good and for His glory. The ministry sign gifts are not only for today; they are for ensuring that life on this planet is demonstrating "on earth as it is in heaven" from the Lord's Prayer (Matthew 6:10).

Healing

The first ministry sign gift is the gift of healing—supernatural intervention to produce physical, spiritual and emotional restoration. People with this gift have a divine enablement to bring healing to others through prayer, touch or speaking words.

I have been part of prayer experiences in which God brought healing to a person through touch. I have also been part of prayer experiences after which sick people worsened and died. In some circumstances, God brings healing through gifted individuals and the prayers of people in faith; in other cases He does not. God is sovereign, and we must rest in His goodness while we are faithful to pray for the sick to be healed even when we do not immediately see the results we desire.

Remember, though, if you get distracted and focus on the gift and not the Giver, you will get misaligned in your spiritual priorities. Our responsibility is to be obedient and pray for healing. Healing is in the Father's hands.

Miracles

The gift of miracles is a supernatural intervention in the spiritual or natural realm. People with this gift can perform acts of supernatural power in order to authenticate the Gospel and give glory to God. Let me give you two examples from the Bible.

The fifth chapter of Mark tells us that Jesus found a man possessed by many demons. The man wore no clothes and was so strong that no chains could bind him. Jesus drove the demons out of the man, and from that point forward, he was "dressed and in his right mind" (Mark 5:15), testifying about Jesus in his region.

An example in the Old Testament occurred in the life of Joshua. During a battle with the Amorites, Joshua prayed to God for the sun to stand still so the Israelites could finish winning their battle against their enemy.

> Joshua said to the LORD in the presence of Israel: "Sun, stand still over Gibeon, and you, moon, over the Valley of Aijalon." So the sun stood still, and the moon stopped, till the nation avenged itself on its enemies.
>
> Joshua 10:12–13

That miracle of God was done through the agency of one of His children.

Does God do miracles every day through His children? You bet! I would never want to say, "That gift is gone. God doesn't do those kinds of miracles anymore." God can do whatever He wants to do and whenever He wants to do it, through whomever He chooses. And I will continue to pray for miracles in the everyday of life.

If events do not happen the way I want them to, I will leave the results to God, because He is in charge; I am not.

Tongues and Interpretation

The last two gifts we will discuss are tongues and interpretation of tongues.

There are two dimensions to the gift of tongues. Although I find Scripture clear about these two aspects, reasonable Christians often disagree on what I am about to share.

The gift of tongues is both a personal prayer language that helps build up a believer's spirit (1 Corinthians 14:14–15; Jude 20) and the supernatural ability to speak in an unlearned language for the purpose of evangelism, such as on the first Day of Pentecost, when three thousand visitors to Jerusalem came to faith in Jesus as a result of hearing "the wonders of God" (Acts 2:11) in their own languages—a book of Acts miracle that still happens today!

I have letters in my files from missionaries facing situations in other countries when they had not yet learned the language of the people they wanted to reach, but God immediately granted them the ability to speak those languages so people would come to know Christ—and they did! God is still using that gift for Kingdom purposes.

People have different beliefs about public expressions of the gift of tongues and interpretation of tongues—interpreting a personal prayer language publicly for the sake of edifying the whole body.

Paul told the church at Corinth to be aware of the presence of unbelievers and to help them not "freak out" (loose translation!) but understand what God is doing and saying (see 1 Corinthians 14:16). Paul went on to say that while the gift of tongues is given to believers, it is often a sign for unbelievers in the assembly (see verses 16 and 22).

Rather than move to the extreme that some churches have, I would never forbid tongues in a public assembly, but ensure through the church leadership that the public exercise of tongues (if and when it happens) is done in such a way as to be understandable to any unbelievers present, all for the sake of the Gospel of Jesus.

Unwrap It, Use It, Develop It

God gave all these gifts to the Church so we could serve Him effectively. God has given *you* a gift, and His gift is a treasure, ready for you to unwrap, if you have not yet done so. He wants you to use it for His glory and honor. If you do not know what your gift is, then find out. If you know what it is but have not been using it, then use it. If you have been using it, then keep developing it.

I would like to share a life-shaping experience from early in my ministry when I was a youth pastor in Buena Park, California, at an old Baptist church. I felt responsible to do home visits with some of the members, and one afternoon I visited Ed Evenson. Ed was a deacon, and he and his wife were older and respected members of the church.

To be honest, I was not looking forward to the visit. I knew that their house would be warm; and I was not sure what an eighteen-year-old youth pastor would talk about with a seventy-something church deacon.

After I arrived and we spoke for about fifteen minutes, Ed asked if he could show me something. He pointed to a thick coffee table–type family Bible. He opened it to the first page, and I saw that it had about ten names written on it. Then he pointed to the second page, and I saw my name there.

Seeing my name in his family Bible was uplifting. But what took my breath away was seeing that the page where my name was written was marked with tears he had wept over the page that very morning.

Writing this some forty-plus years later still brings moisture to my eyes. I have mentioned Ed Evenson and his prayers for me many times publicly. When I get to see Ed in the presence of Jesus, I will run up to him and give him a bear hug and love on him like crazy. Then I will ask the Father if He will show the video of how many times the prayers of Ed and others have covered me and prevented evil from taking root in my life.

Why am I sharing this with you? Because every person in your church family, every person in the Body of Christ, and every person who has ever been reached for Jesus has a special gifting and assignment in His Body. I am praying that you are part of the great revolution of helping every follower of Jesus find his or her place in His Kingdom work.

And my great hope is that this brief overview of spiritual gifts will stimulate you to discover and use your own spiritual gifts to fulfill His Kingdom assignment for you.

The next chapter will activate us, and we will begin to see how the people of God can establish transformational breakthroughs by bringing heaven to earth and distributing grace in culture.

Below I have provided links to resources that you can study further and take tests to help you discern your spiritual gifts.

BEFORE YOU GO

Do you know your spiritual gifts? Would you be comfortable describing your identity in Christ (who you are), your spiritual gifts (what He has given you), and your sense of assignment in the Kingdom (what He has called you to do)? When you are using your spiritual gifts, what do you experience? Do you feel that others recognize and affirm your gifts?

There are a number of online spiritual gifts assessment tools. Following are links to sites where you can find resources or actually take an inventory to discover your spiritual gifts:

- Ministry Tools Resource Center: An online spiritual gifts test inventory assessment at http://mintools.com/spiritual-gifts-test.htm.
- Eleven Talents Ministry: A spiritual gifts test at https://www.mycornerstone.org/wp-content/uploads /spiritualgiftstest.pdf.
- Team Ministry: A spiritual gifts analysis at http:// www.churchgrowth.org/cgi-cg/gifts.cgi?intro=1.
- Lay Ministry: A downloadable spiritual gifts test and workbook at http://www.layministry.com/.
- My seminary professor, C. Peter Wagner, wrote some excellent books on spiritual gifts, which you can find here: http://bakerpublishinggroup.com/chosen/l/finding -spiritual-gifts.

10

GRACE IN THE MARKETPLACE

James and Rebecca seemed to be hitting their stride. Their two children were now ages seven and four, with a third (and maybe final!) child on the way. Rebecca worked on freelance projects from home, and their son, still precocious and increasingly analytical, was learning a lot as Rebecca homeschooled him with James's assistance. Their four-year-old daughter was sometimes jealous of her big brother, so Rebecca provided some early school-like experiences for her.

James loved seeing the family learning together. In fact, he was also learning some exciting things at work. A couple of promotions and the opportunity to earn a certificate in project management meant that James was conversing more with team members and relating to people from various departments. It fascinated him how often these conversations bordered on spiritual sensitivities, and James prayed about how to share his faith in Christ and spiritual life with his colleagues.

My hope in the next few pages is to "shock" you with a different view of your job. I believe in the power of the marketplace. I think leaders in business, education, health care, media, the arts and government all have the capacity to influence the future of our world for Kingdom purposes—or the opposite.

Sadly, as we have seen, many in the Church have bought into the lie that the "secular" world of the marketplace is evil and only the Church is holy. This has meant, tragically, that many spiritual leaders have abandoned the marketplace—as well as the believers who work in it and contribute to it—in the belief that it is "unspiritual."

Eminent sociologist Rodney Stark caused quite a stir when his study of ancient history led him to describe Western foundations as follows: "The success of the West, including the rise of science, rested entirely on religious foundations, and the people who brought it about were devout Christians."[1]

Rather than avoid the marketplace, I believe that grace ambassadors who understand their calling will position themselves to lead and invest in marketplace spheres for Kingdom purposes.

Kingdom Assignments

I had the privilege of launching John Maxwell's "Million Leader Mandate" equipping the work of ministry in the nation of Kenya. Over a number of years, I made repeated trips to that East African nation to work with bishops and pastors, who would then teach others. I loved being with those leaders. But a special and initially unplanned part of my trips was a series of regular meetings with marketplace, educational and governmental leaders.

Over several years and multiple trips, I had the joy of teaching and sharing with Jesus-loving men and women with a calling to full-time vocational assignments. The ministry assignments of these men and women were not primarily in the Church gathered (although they all served in their local churches). But the fruit of their ministry in the marketplace of life was amazing!

One of these dedicated participants served as a vice president for a multinational company, living out his life faithfully as a disciple of Christ in the corporate realm. His wife was a leading discipler of women. She had deep and rich biblical knowledge and manifested the fruit of the Spirit in the community relationships she had carefully nurtured over the years. Both of them were living as grace ambassadors bringing heaven to earth!

Why was this experience so unusual for me? Because for many years I had the traditional thinking pattern that only those who worked full time for our church were in "vocational ministry." Like many others in vocational ministry, I often saw the women and men in the churches I pastored who worked "regular jobs" as heroic but not in full-time ministry. Sadly, this line of thinking actually had me perpetuating the sacred/secular divide, where I believed that those who worked in vocational ministry were perhaps a little less "stained" by the culture of the world, and (at my worst!) maybe even a little more sanctified.

That sacred/secular divide is real in the thinking and behavior of many of us. But my trips to Kenya gave me the opportunity to revise my thinking and ask the Lord for wisdom on how to change the mindsets of vocational ministry leaders and men and women in the marketplace.

More recently I have had the experience at William Jessup University[2] of working with wonderful people in our community and on our board of trustees who serve in dynamic and sometimes powerful marketplace, governmental and educational settings as ambassadors of heaven. (The board chair for my first five years at the university, for example, was Patrick P. Gelsinger, current CEO of Intel.)

What is the problem and how do we overcome it? The problem is that we who are pastors and leaders and missionaries have often appeared to suggest that pastoral and missionary work is the highest calling (or the only calling), and that anyone not called to ministry work for the Church gathered is left with a second-class assignment. Part of activating the second Reformation and bringing heaven to earth is for leaders to repent personally and on behalf of the Body of Christ for this wrong understanding and teaching.

Something the Lord led me to do in Kenya, which I have since repeated in the United States and England, is to repent of what I personally, and we in leadership, have taught and modeled in error about the Church (*ekklesia*) and the Kingdom. Each time I have repented of this kind of teaching or have led a group of pastors to repent of this kind of teaching, I have sensed release in the meeting as brothers and sisters who have longed for a sense of calling in the marketplace felt freed and blessed to soar into their Kingdom assignments.

Honoring and equipping the Church distributed is a critical foundation stone for the ministry of the Holy Spirit to be released in the educational, governmental and marketplace spheres through discipled and called men and women.

Kingdom Ambassadors

I mentioned in chapter 1 that my father was a Baptist minister. Dad had a strong sense of call to the pastoral ministry. But in the churches in which I grew up, there was a huge gulf between the pastors and missionaries and the rest of the people. So when I began pastoring, I felt a strong call to honor and affirm the marketplace (despite my erroneous worldviews about vocational ministry) and to be engaged in the community I served.

Later in my life, the writings of my friend Ed Silvoso helped me develop a language and theology of the marketplace.

In his book *Anointed for Business*, Silvoso outlines four "lethal misbeliefs" that derail a complete view of what Kingdom ministry can look like in the marketplace. This combination of major misbeliefs usually neutralizes God's calling on those anointed for marketplace ministry:

1. There is a God-ordained division between clergy and laity.
2. The Church is called to operate primarily inside a building often referred to as the temple.
3. People involved in business cannot be as spiritual as those serving in traditional church ministry.
4. The primary role of marketplace Christians is to make money to support the vision of those "in the ministry."[3]

I am convinced that the Lord is raising up a generation of ministry leaders who will recognize, call forth, equip and release men and women to their assignment as the Church distributed. Part of my own personal discipline is to say something like this in front of a crowd of marketplace leaders:

"Your vocation is not a curse; it is a calling. You are Kingdom ambassadors in the marketplaces of life, and the Spirit of God has called and equipped you to serve Him faithfully in whatever corridors you travel. You are ambassadors of heaven, and you serve with authority and with credentials on behalf of the King himself. You are the Church distributed."

The Holy Spirit has often used this statement, followed by a prayer of confession, blessing and release, to embolden and empower gatherings of Kingdom believers.

A New Testament passage often used for apologetics purposes is a clarion call for every follower of Jesus who longs to bring heaven to earth:

> In your hearts revere Christ as Lord. Always be prepared to give an answer to everyone who asks you to give the reason for the hope that you have. But do this with gentleness and respect, keeping a clear conscience, so that those who speak maliciously against your good behavior in Christ may be ashamed of their slander.
>
> 1 Peter 3:15–16

The fivefold ministry must also equip the Body of Christ, so that we are not only saved from hell, but sanctified for serving the Lord, and so we can answer and reach those who have not yet come to know the love of the Savior.

Spirit-empowered believers, who are the Church distributed, operating in the marketplace as heavenly ambassadors, will inaugurate the second Reformation as they carry the presence of heaven to spheres of influence where the Church gathered can never reach.

In his book *Love Does*, Christian author Bob Goff puts it this way:

> I've met people . . . who leak Jesus. Whenever you're around them, Jesus keeps coming up with words and with actions. I don't suppose everybody gets hit by Jesus, but those of

us who have, talk about Him differently. We start steering funny; we start leaking where we stand.[4]

Reimagining Leadership

I have been grappling with this framework for years, and determined that I had to change my sense of my own role and the work of the ministry. Throughout the course of my pastoral and leadership ministry, this meant that I have had to reimagine the leadership paradigm that is most common.

Some years ago, while working with those key leaders in Kenya, I drew two diagrams that I have found useful to this day. I would like to share them with you and then unpack how the concepts work in equipping marketplace leaders in your church or ministry.

This first diagram seeks to attack the heart of how many of us in leadership have been trained:

TWO VIEWS OF LEADERSHIP STRATEGY

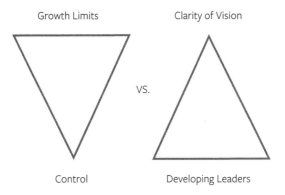

The drawing on the left (the inverted triangle) demonstrates how most of us operate. We establish strong elements of control—us, our policies, our structures—that unintentionally constrain or limit our ability to grow.

The drawing on the right suggests that if we have clarity of vision, and the corresponding cultural values of our organization or ministry aligned, then our only limitation is the ability to develop leaders.

The simplicity of this drawing is what draws people to its truth. Most leaders, whether knowingly or unknowingly, have established points of control that constrict the ability of people in their ministries or organizations to flourish and mature. We limit creativity and development by stunting people into rigid boxes that we have made. The drawing on the right describes the atmosphere and culture that exist when we have clarity of vision and a systematic, intentional process for identifying, training and releasing leaders to their Kingdom assignments.

Through the years I have spoken to many highly placed and gifted leaders in a variety of vocational settings who were essentially told that they could give money or serve in a support role, but they were never allowed to maximize their gifts in the Church gathered. This must stop! We need to equip, bless and release the gifts of God's people so the Church gathered receives from all its members, including those strategically placed in culture; *and* we need to bless, release and support men and women in their public assignments to be the Church distributed in their schools, businesses, governmental agencies or wherever they are serving.

In this new season, the Spirit is calling us to develop Kingdom leaders. There are literally generals and captains waiting to be equipped and mobilized to bring heaven to earth who are sitting in the seats of the Church gathered without authorization or ambassadorship. We must get the people of God moving across the cultural streams with the redemptive heart of the Father.

PASTORPRENEUR

This second diagram has been used with church planters and pastors across the U.S. and England and Africa. The calling of God must be rooted in the heart of the pastor/ leader whom God has raised up for the community. The calling (or encounter) that we have from God will almost certainly become a defining experience and life mission that grips our hearts. Then the leader gains understanding—like the tribe of Issachar, "who understood the times and knew what Israel should do" (1 Chronicles 12:32)—of what the community needs.

There is a moment when we understand the times and know what to do. At this point many leaders will start making plans.

But I think there is another step, which is to say, *Lord, whom have You entrusted to me?* Recognizing the gifts of the women and men God has called to the team may mean a radical shift in how the ministry responds to the calling of God and to the needs of the community. Pastors and leaders have an opportunity to call forth the individuals and individual gifts the Lord has provided so the ministry expands beyond anything possible on a human scale.

In this season we are seeing a movement of "Grace Ambassador: Bringing Heaven to Earth" in which the fivefold ministry steps into a special and sanctified partnership with the other members of the Body of Christ in order to equip and call forth the 90 percent who have been wondering what their assignment is in the Body. I am preparing and celebrating in advance what an activated Body looks like as we see men and women experiencing the fullness of His calling and gifting in all the spheres of society.

This is not an exact science, but I have long believed (and sought to practice!) that if 100 percent of the people in a local church family could be mobilized, only 20 percent would be needed for the ministries of the Church gathered and 80 percent could be equipped and released for redemptive presence ministry in the community as the Church distributed. I pray that many local churches and leaders will press in for this type of release.

When I think of grace being released in communities through equipped and transformed men and women, I imagine heaven on earth! When the people of God are equipped and released, the *ekklesia* will begin to transform culture as we move from intimacy and empowerment to expression and engagement with the culture. This movement will bring heaven to earth—a glorious moment as we see grace distributed by the people of God where He has established them.

The Church gathered has innate limitations on who and how many she can reach. The Church distributed carries the presence of Jesus into every sphere of society and culture. The intersection of personal revival and cultural transformation happens when Jesus' followers are equipped and empowered to bless the nations in their everyday lives.

In the next chapter, I hope to help you be an ambassador of heaven and reach the world He has called you to.

BEFORE YOU GO

Have you ever thought of your job as an assignment from God? Have you ever wondered if the neighborhood you live in is not an accident, but rather, if your address is your assignment? Do you wonder why you sometimes feel like the only Christian at work, in your gym or in your family? What would it look like for you to carry the grace of God to your family, neighborhood or workplace?

11

SHARING GRACE
WITH OUR WORLD

Jim and Rebecca had a challenge. Jim had recently been sharing more openly with two guys at work about his faith, and the conversation was getting deep. But Jim told Rebecca he felt inadequate to relay both the "what" and the "why" of his faith. He knew what he had experienced in his relationship with God, but he was unclear about how to communicate it effectively with others. His friends were at least open, but not yet willing to come to church.

So Jim and Rebecca decided to meet the challenge by inviting these two co-workers and their wives over for dinner.

Before they did, they asked their pastor to help them get ready to share their faith in a more intentional and effective fashion.

I once saw a Peanuts cartoon with Lucy saying to Charlie Brown, "I hate everything. I hate everybody. I hate the whole wide world!" Charlie Brown says, "But I thought you had inner peace." Lucy replies, "I do have inner peace. But I still have outer obnoxiousness."

Sadly, some in the Body of Christ have become so angry and disengaged from our culture that we have a bit of the "Lucy" atmosphere around us. We may feel we have inner peace, yet we are perceived by the world around us as having outer obnoxiousness. In fact, many in the world think that followers of Jesus see themselves as superior to normal people in society.

It is true that some measure of that picture has been painted by a contrary media climate, but there is also a sense in which we followers of Christ have determined that our battle is with the people we live near or work with each day. Contrast this view with Paul's admonition to the Colossians:

> Be wise in the way you act toward outsiders; make the most of every opportunity. Let your conversation be always full of grace, seasoned with salt, so that you may know how to answer everyone.
>
> Colossians 4:5–6

I would like for us take up a challenge on our journey: What does it look like for the people of God—for you and me—to be full of grace in a way that makes people hungry for Him? Specifically, if the Church gathered worships the Lord of all creation, and the Church distributed carries His presence and grace to every realm of that same creation, what does that look like in the modern world of cultural influence? How can we share with our culture, lovingly and with truth and compassion, about the life and love of Jesus?

Principles of Ambassadorship

Let me present a biblical framework to strengthen the foundation we have built. How do we go about our heavenly ambassadorship of bringing heaven to earth?

Here are some principles to get us moving in the right direction.

Walk in Authority

Bringing heaven to earth requires that we recognize the fundamentally spiritual nature of our battle and the practice of sharing grace in real life every day.

We are ambassadors in the midst of a war for which the outcome is already determined—so we wage war from the position of victory and authority.

> Be strong in the Lord and in his mighty power. Put on the full armor of God, so that you can take your stand against the devil's schemes. For our struggle is not against flesh and blood, but against the rulers, against the authorities, against the powers of this dark world and against the spiritual forces of evil in the heavenly realms.
>
> Ephesians 6:10–12 (see also
2 Corinthians 10:4–5)

It is dangerous to fail to recognize that we are in a time of deep spiritual conflict. As challenging as the spiritual atmosphere is in our present world, we must settle it firmly in our hearts that Satan is defeated and that he has no "legal" power or authority on his own. All he has are the authority and rights we give him by subjecting our will, authority and rights as members of the human race to his demonic control. If all of us stopped cooperating with him and listening to him, he and his minions would be ineffective.

We walk in authority; and everything we do in our lives as blood-bought sons and daughters of the Almighty is through the power of the Spirit, the same Spirit who raised Jesus from the dead.

Live in the Overflow

The Jesus life is abundant and full; we live in the overflow of grace.

> Just as you received Christ Jesus as Lord, continue to live your lives in him, rooted and built up in him, strengthened in the faith as you were taught, and overflowing with thankfulness.
>
> Colossians 2:6–7

Our lives represent a continuous flow of relational intimacy in which Jesus lives and breathes and moves in and through us. We are the life and grace of Jesus as we walk and talk. He calls us to Himself. And when we have an encounter with Him, the overflow is a naturally supernatural experience that will result in love and kindness to those with whom we interact.

Demonstrate Love

We bring heaven to earth through demonstrating the love of God manifested in the everyday, including to people who feel far from Him. We love others because of the love Jesus has demonstrated to us. New Testament Christianity recognizes each disciple of Jesus as an equipped ambassador who brings heaven to earth in his or her daily life, relationships and workplace settings, in response to what Jesus has done for us. We live in the world with redemptive presence as heavenly ambassadors and grace distributors.

The concept and reality of grace is like a sumo wrestler—hard to get your arms around! But when I think of grace as God's love manifested in the everyday, I get a clearer picture, seeing not only Jesus our Savior on the cross, but followers of Jesus who demonstrate love and compassion in His name (see Matthew 25 for one such description).

Recognize Amazing Grace

Our relationship with God is based on our faith in the finished work of Jesus Christ on the cross for our salvation and healing. Salvation brings us peace with God. As believers in Christ, we must recognize that we stand in His presence only through the grace of God (see Romans 5:1–2).

In fact, it is grace that sets Christianity apart from all other religions. John R. W. Stott made this observation regarding the difference between the Christian faith and Islam:

> The repeated promises in the Qur'an of the forgiveness of a compassionate and merciful Allah are all made to the meritorious, whose merits have been weighed on Allah's scales, whereas the gospel is good news of mercy to the undeserving. The symbol of the religion of Jesus is the cross, not the scales.[1]

Once we understand the truly amazing nature of grace—John Newton, a former slave trader who became a pastor, wrote the hymn "Amazing Grace" because he recognized it!—our natural response is to respond to that grace by giving to others what has been given to us.

When Pam and I got married, we wanted to put a Scripture on our wedding invitation. We finally settled on 1 John 4:19: "We love because he first loved us." God is the "first mover." He demonstrated His love for us by showing us grace; our response must be to receive it and share it with others!

It is absolutely imperative to recognize that our response to grace does *not* mean that we have somehow "earned" it. No, grace is what we receive undeservedly. And our response is what we give freely. Ephesians 2:8–10 describes the sequence in clear terms:

> It is by grace you have been saved, through faith—and this is not from yourselves, it is the gift of God—not by works, so that no one can boast. For we are God's handiwork, created in Christ Jesus to do good works, which God prepared in advance for us to do.

All of us who have come to know Jesus as Savior have received the grace of salvation and the gift of the Spirit by His unmerited kindness. Our response should be to live as a redemptive presence in the world and to be a grace distributor on earth on behalf of the King.

The Prodigal Brother

Before we talk about this further, I think we need to be honest right here in the family. Many of us, having received grace, are frustrated and even angry at others who stand in desperate need of the gift we have already accepted. Let's use a well-known parable as a way to illustrate this important lesson.

Almost everyone likes a party. Almost no one associates Christianity with a party, but Jesus did. He talked about the rejoicing that goes on in heaven when a sinner repents, about the Kingdom of heaven being like a king who holds a great feast and about heaven being like a wedding supper.

The Bible is full of the imagery of parties—but it is possible to miss the party. Jesus tells us how at the end of the Parable of the Prodigal Son.

The younger brother takes his inheritance and wastes it in a far country. He trades his self-respect for a pigpen. There he learns a great lesson: Life can begin in a disaster that reveals our need for God.

The wandering, shivering, hungry boy returns penniless, having abused his father's kindness, now willing to become a servant in his house. But when the father sees him in the distance, he runs to greet him. And before the boy can deliver his well-rehearsed speech, he is wrapped up in his father's grace. Ecstatic to see his son, the father kills the prized calf and hosts a party, with music and dancing.

Let's pick up Jesus' story at this point:

"The older son was in the field. When he came near the house, he heard music and dancing. So he called one of the servants and asked him what was going on. 'Your brother has come,' he replied, 'and your father has killed the fattened calf because he has him back safe and sound.'

"The older brother became angry and refused to go in. So his father went out and pleaded with him. But he answered his father, 'Look! All these years I've been slaving for you and never disobeyed your orders. Yet you never gave me even a young goat so I could celebrate with my friends. But when this son of yours who has squandered your property with prostitutes comes home, you kill the fattened calf for him!'

"'My son,' the father said, 'you are always with me, and everything I have is yours. But we had to celebrate and be glad, because this brother of yours was dead and is alive again; he was lost and is found.'"

Luke 15:25–32

The older son who came out of the field but refused to go in is now a prodigal of sorts himself. One son ran away from home; the other refused to go home. Outside the house is outside the house, regardless of how one gets there. The older brother missed the party. Why? And further, why do some of us have "older brother faith"?

On the one hand, it is perfectly understandable to see the older brother's anger. He did not understand his father's response to his brother. After all, it does seem like a raw deal. While the younger son was sowing wild oats, the older son was sowing the crops. How could the father be so kind to the undeserving? No doubt he said to himself, *So this is how you get recognition in this house. Run away, waste money, drink and party.* Rather than celebrate his father's kindness as a virtue, he condemned it as a vice.

The more I have thought about this in my own life, born and raised in the church as a Baptist pastor's son, I have felt convicted about my own "older brother faith." This quote from Robert Farrar Capon about the story brought me to a full stop:

> You're worried about permissiveness—about the way the preaching of grace seems to say it's okay to do all kinds of terrible things as long as you just walk in afterward and take the free gift of God's forgiveness. While you and I may be worried about seeming to give permission, Jesus apparently wasn't. He wasn't afraid of giving the prodigal son a kiss instead of a lecture, a party instead of probation; and he proved that by bringing in the elder brother at the end of the story and having him raise pretty much the same objections you do. He's angry about the party. He complains that his father is lowering standards and ignoring virtue—that music, dancing and a fattened calf are, in effect, just so many permissions to break the law. And to that, Jesus has the

father say only one thing: "Cut that out! We're not playing good boys and bad boys anymore. Your brother was dead and he's alive again. The name of the game from now on is resurrection, not bookkeeping."[2]

The older brother also did not understand or accept his brother's transformation. The younger brother really was a changed man. He exhibited real repentance. It took a lot to admit he was wrong. He did not come home demanding, but begging. He left home saying, "Give me"; he came home saying, "Forgive me." But the older brother could not accept that.

Like him, we must look for repentance in others. But I have to admit, I am often unwilling to see it because it is not on my terms.

Finally, the older brother did not understand his own reality. Nothing he had would be taken away. Whatever privileges he had were still his. He never had to go hungry. He never had to face the degradation of the far country. Righteousness has its own rewards.

But although his behavior was "good," there was a problem in his heart that can only be described as sin. He, too, needed to depend on his father's mercy. The party was a celebration of grace—a gift he, too, could receive. Sadly, however, he was so angry he missed all the fun.

He was not, however, shut out of the banquet hall. He locked himself out. The father wanted him to come in. He probably did not even realize that a place was set at the table for him. There was a plate filled for him. They probably saved him a piece of cake, if only he had the sense to go in.

Changing the Culture

Our mandate is learning to receive God's grace, embrace it in our own lives and bring heaven to earth as grace distributors for the King of the universe.

Paul, a Pharisee who had killed followers of Jesus in his earlier zeal to follow his religious upbringing, described his own journey with grace in this way:

> By the grace of God I am what I am, and his grace to me was not without effect. No, I worked harder than all of them—yet not I, but the grace of God that was with me.
>
> 1 Corinthians 15:10

When I speak in local churches, I sometimes say, "Christians are mean, angry, judgmental and condemning." Often I will say it twice, and then let the words hang in the air.

On most occasions the silence and frustration in the room are palpable.

Then I say, "Actually, I do not think that about you. I know that is not who you are as followers of Jesus. But I want you to know what many in the world system have been led to believe about you."

I long for that narrative to be replaced by another one. What would it be like to hear it said that Christians are loving, forgiving, peaceful and hopeful? Imagine family, neighbors, co-workers and the general public recognizing that the caricature they have been sold about real-life, flesh-and-blood Jesus followers is all wrong!

The presence of Jesus followers in every setting of society as loving, forgiving, peaceful and hopeful would change the atmosphere of culture! Imagine the receptivity of people to the Savior if they experienced Jesus followers this way.

The apostle Paul already did: "All this is for your benefit," he wrote, "so that the grace that is reaching more and more people may cause thanksgiving to overflow to the glory of God" (2 Corinthians 4:15).

Revival begins in the household of faith. Reformation takes place in the culture as redeemed and revived servants of the Most High live in power and redemptive grace to extend love, forgiveness, peace and hope to our world.

I am convinced that increasing numbers of what I sometimes call grace distributorships will open up around the world, staffed by followers of Jesus who love Him and love the people He died for.

As the second Reformation is manifested in the Church gathered and distributed, the transformation of culture will happen. This is the vision of the movement to bring heaven to earth.

BEFORE YOU GO

Have you had the experience of trying to share your faith with someone who was angry at Christians and Christianity? Have you ever tried to share your relationship with Christ and felt at a loss for words, or at a loss for how to reach the person or group? Do you feel confident in being used by the Holy Spirit to reach people who do not yet know Christ? Or do you feel uncertain?

12

THE SPIRITUAL WAR OVER GRACE

It was exciting and heartbreaking at the same time! When Enrique first heard James describe his growing faith, he appeared uninterested. But after a few interactions, Enrique began having more consistent conversations with James. Finally, after attending church with James a few times, Enrique came to him one day at work with what seemed to be a whole new countenance. He had opened his heart to God, he told James, and asked Jesus to be ruler of his life. He said he wanted help to live his life in alignment with God and His truth.

At the same time, other co-workers became increasingly hostile to James—and to Enrique as well, once Enrique began to share his spiritual journey. It became apparent that James and Enrique were being mistrusted and even targeted by some of their friends at work who had once seemed like a band of brothers. Although neither of them realized it, the spiritual atmosphere at work had shifted. Hostility toward faith and spiritual life was now very real and evident.

What happens when the one Jesus described as "the thief [who] comes only to steal and kill and destroy" (John 10:10) begins to lose souls, territory and dominion as his targets are transformed by the grace of God? What happens when people recognize the kindness of God through Kingdom grace distributors and come to personal repentance (see Romans 2:4)?

Opposition. The history of the Church suggests that Satan, the enemy of our souls, resists revival and reformation. In fact, the last decade has seen an increase in the activity of demonic forces as our adversary gains ground in the sphere of culture while simultaneously sensing that his time on earth is drawing to a close. Spiritual intensity in our time seems to have increased dramatically. Warfare is now more prevalent and tangible.

Although Jesus said that "the gates of hell shall not prevail against" His Church (Matthew 16:18 KJV), recent events have caused many of us to question that assertion. The combination of political polarization, racial injustice, social inequality, and a global pandemic fueling economic uncertainty has caused many believers to retreat in fear from the chaos of the cultural moment.

At the same time, the Church is beginning to rise up. The Father is calling forth a generation of Spirit-empowered followers of Jesus as heavenly ambassadors into every sphere of society.

Jesus taught that there is tremendous power when His children—us!—agree on earth. He said, "Truly I tell you that if two of you on earth agree about anything they ask for, it will be done for them by my Father in heaven" (Matthew 18:19). In my own journey of faith, since agreement on earth can move heaven, I have come increasingly to believe and experience the power that comes about when we say or write something, then have other believers join together in agreement. Think of how a crowd cheering at an athletic contest makes everyone feel. Now imagine what happens when the whole Church comes together and makes declarations about who we are and what we are called to do here on this planet and in this time period.

In that spirit, then, I am contending for a prevailing Church. On the authority of the words of Jesus and in the power of His resurrection, I am declaring that the era of a passive, weak, disengaged, fear-filled Church is over. The people of God are waking up, rising up and being stirred up for battle against the enemy! Although he is indeed the thief of John 10:10, and although he "prowls around like a roaring lion" (1 Peter 5:8), we declare that the only Lion who matters is "the Lion of the tribe of Judah" (Revelation 5:5), whose name is Jesus.

The remnant Church is beginning to heed the call of Matthew 5:13–16 to be salt and light. That admonition and the promises of Isaiah 58 are the clarion calls of our time. You may be less familiar with the prophetic exhortation of Isaiah 58, so I reprint a portion of it here:

> "Is not this the kind of fasting I have chosen: to loose the chains of injustice and untie the cords of the yoke, to set the oppressed free and break every yoke? Is it not to share your food with the hungry and to provide the poor wanderer with shelter—when you see the naked, to clothe them, and not to turn away from your own flesh and blood? Then your light

will break forth like the dawn, and your healing will quickly appear; then your righteousness will go before you, and the glory of the LORD will be your rear guard. Then you will call, and the LORD will answer; you will cry for help, and he will say: Here am I.

"If you do away with the yoke of oppression, with the pointing finger and malicious talk, and if you spend yourselves in behalf of the hungry and satisfy the needs of the oppressed, then your light will rise in the darkness, and your night will become like the noonday. The LORD will guide you always; he will satisfy your needs in a sun-scorched land and will strengthen your frame. You will be like a well-watered garden, like a spring whose waters never fail. Your people will rebuild the ancient ruins and will raise up the age-old foundations; you will be called Repairer of Broken Walls, Restorer of Streets with Dwellings."

verses 6–12

Receive that declaration! When we walk in alignment with that word, and when our culture sees us bringing heaven to earth, we will bring love, forgiveness, peace and hope to communities across the planet.

Can you imagine what will happen in every culture when cities and regions and nations flourish, recognizing that followers of Jesus are leading the reformation? What an exciting time to be alive! I can see you, dear reader, as part of the movement that reshapes families, organizations, communities and nations with the power and presence of Christ in the power of the Holy Spirit. This is a vision of the people of God that stirs the heart and galvanizes us to fulfill His Kingdom assignment where He has placed us.

Sadly, many in the Body of Christ have withdrawn from the battlefield and waved the flag of surrender. We have believed the lie that the public square or private marketplace is too dangerous a place for Jesus followers. We have kept quiet about our faith at work, at school, at the arts, in sports and sometimes even at home. We have been ruled by the fear of "giants in the land."

Five Smooth Stones for the Church

Thousands of years ago a shepherd boy faced a giant. The army behind the boy had cowered in fear as they saw and heard the giant shouting at them from the other side of the valley. The shepherd boy was offended that this giant had been challenging the army of God without response for days. He was eager to take him on. But instead of putting on the weapons of traditional warfare—armor and helmet and sword—the shepherd boy picked out five smooth stones to fit into his slingshot.

David killed the cursing giant and had one of history's greatest victories in a story that has been told and retold for three thousand years.

Jesus followers who bring His grace to culture are like David, the shepherd boy who became king. We face the giants of our own time. Like David, we are called to be leading and shaping culture, not fearing the battle and retreating.

I have sensed a number of very challenging areas of spiritual warfare in recent years. It is a deeply held burden of my heart to see Jesus followers bring grace and truth to the issues of our day, including historical revisionism, abortion and euthanasia, religious repression, racism and injustice, identity and family. God is calling His people to establish a clear and compelling framework for revival and reformation. In each case we need to make affirmative declarations and live out our faith in the everyday circumstances of life.

What I call "Five Smooth Stones for the Church" are part of what I see as the calling of grace ambassadors in our current cultural milieu:

Foundations: We are committed to biblical authority in life, and we pray that our nation will live in alignment with the will of God so we can see our nation bring glory to God through our national character.

Life: We are committed to treating all human life as precious and made in the image of God. We honor life in the womb and outside the womb until natural death.

Liberty: We are committed to religious and economic liberty, and we believe that repressive economic and political governmental systems destroy the freedom God intends for people living on earth.

Justice: We are committed to a biblical experience of racial unity and justice, applying grace and truth to reforming health care, immigration and the criminal justice systems.

Family: We are committed to biblical views of gender, sexuality, marriage and family, in which parents have the right and responsibility to protect children from harmful decisions and inputs.

Believing and Contending

I have written more fully about current cultural climate responses in my book *The Prevailing Church* (Jessup University Press, 2021). When we shine the light of Christ into dark places, the enemy will indeed respond—but we have the full protection of Jesus.

Sadly, as I have said, many of us cower in fear while stepping outside the atmosphere of the Church, while the Gospel of Jesus calls us into open confrontation with the powers of darkness in every sphere of life.

Ed Stetzer, a professor and dean at Wheaton College, describes it this way in his powerful book *Subversive Kingdom*:

> Through Jesus' teaching and preaching, he was proclaiming to everyone that they could be part of God's agenda on earth by repenting and believing, that this "kingdom of heaven" was primarily spiritual in nature. And through his miracles of healing, he was making visibly evident his authoritative power over the curse of our fallen, helpless condition. After all, "Which is easier: to say to the paralytic, 'Your sins are forgiven,' or to say, 'Get up, pick up your mat and walk'?" (Mark 2:9). They're both easy when your power as King is supreme over every part of the rebellious world, both physical and spiritual.[1]

While the enemy of our souls comes to "steal and kill and destroy" (John 10:10, the verse we quoted at the beginning of this chapter), Jesus declares in the same verse, "I have come that they may have life, and have it to the full." We can live this abundant life in the victorious and prevailing power of the Holy Spirit.

Our mission to bring heaven to earth includes a call to engage the enemy, but not on his territory. We war "not against flesh and blood" (Ephesians 6:12), and not using the tools and weapons of the enemy, but with the weapons of the Spirit (see 2 Corinthians 10:3–5). In this critical time in human history, Jesus calls His followers to live the abundant life well beyond our church walls, bringing the Kingdom of God to the zip codes of the world.

Reggie McNeal describes it this way in his book *Missional Renaissance*:

When the Church thinks it's the destination, it also confuses the scorecard. It thinks that if people are hovering around and in the Church, the Church is winning. The truth is, when that's the case, the Church is really keeping people from where they want to go, from their real destination. The destination is life. Abundant life is lived out with loved ones, friends and acquaintances in the marketplace, in the home, in the neighborhood, in the world.[2]

Both Stetzer and McNeal challenge us again with our definition of success in ministry. Are we content to believe that the number of people attending our gatherings is the singular indicator of spiritual victory? The New Testament records the number of people at particular gatherings (for example, in Acts 2 and Acts 4), but in the vast majority of Acts and the epistles, the stories center on teachings about spiritual maturity, holiness and spiritual warfare.

I believe we have lost sight of the fundamental reality of the spiritual atmosphere in which we operate. The enemy of our souls has been able to lull us into a form of complacency that makes us irrelevant to the Father's Kingdom agenda.

Let's believe and contend instead as Spirit-filled Christians to live as grace distributors, bringing heaven to earth in the relationships and marketplaces of life, for the glory of the name of Jesus.

The second Reformation will come as revival spreads from individuals to families to communities to regions. You can become part of an exponential move of God. That is the topic of our next chapter.

BEFORE YOU GO

Have you experienced a shift in the spiritual atmosphere? What are some of the indicators that spiritual forces are opposing your own growth in Christ? Have you joined others to pray about the spiritual realities you are facing? If you doubt that spiritual warfare is real, reread Ephesians 6:10–20. When you face spiritual opposition, be sure to reach out to trusted friends. Do not walk alone into the battle!

13

HOW FAITH AND LIFE
INTERSECT FOR REVIVAL

James and Rebecca had experienced several years of increasing spiritual growth. The presence of the Lord and the power of the Holy Spirit now felt far beyond words on a page. As they read Scripture, prayed, worshiped and walked through a normal day, they sensed the presence of the Lord with them. Their pastors and church friends kept affirming their respective gifts, and James and Rebecca felt increasingly that their family, their friends, their work and their everyday world were all part of the spiritual adventure they had been given to live.

Even more exciting was that their children were growing in their faith and that their co-workers seemed increasingly responsive to the good news of Jesus. After Enrique had opened his heart to God, several others in James's workplace had been won, after their initial hostility, by the two men's patience and sincerity, and had also responded to the love of Christ. Times of prayer and ekklesia at work were growing. Rebecca, still freelancing, and with more freedom now that the children were a bit older, was ministering to several women in the neighborhood, who had experienced breakthrough in some personally challenging circumstances. All this was happening as the days seemed to fly by—their oldest was now on the edge of being a teenager—and their prayers were intensifying.

The Church gathered—equipped and released to bring heaven to earth as distributors of grace—will bring revival and transformation to our world. The Church distributed continues to operate as a relational community; we are witness to the trinitarian nature of God as we live to the praise and glory of the Father and magnify the Son by the power of the Spirit. This happens in our everyday world as we love, live and work.

Pastor Jack Hayford, founding pastor of The Church On The Way in Van Nuys, California, has been a long-distance mentor to me for years, and I have had the honor to be with him in a number of settings. When he spoke at our university commencement, he challenged us to understand that a prophecy Isaiah gave to Judah and Jerusalem is also a promise for the life of the Church:

> Now it will come about that in the last days the mountain of the house of the LORD will be established as the chief of the mountains, and will be raised above the hills.
>
> Isaiah 2:2 NASB

As I have said many times, it is *Go!* time for the Church to be full of the presence of Jesus and to release His love and grace into our world.

As Pastor Jack said, Isaiah 2 will be fulfilled as the "mountain of the house of the LORD"—His people, the Church—will be lifted above all other mountains, and we will be a blessing to the people. Isaiah 58 declared prophetically that we will be repairers of the breach and restorers of the wall. And we will walk in fulfillment of Isaiah 61, as the people of God distribute the grace and kindness of the Lord. We will fulfill what Jesus declared as He read from the scroll:

> The Spirit of the Sovereign LORD is on me, because the LORD has anointed me to proclaim good news to the poor. He has sent me to bind up the brokenhearted, to proclaim freedom for the captives and release from darkness for the prisoners, to proclaim the year of the LORD's favor and the day of vengeance of our God, to comfort all who mourn, and provide for those who grieve in Zion—to bestow on them a crown of beauty instead of ashes, the oil of joy instead of mourning, and a garment of praise instead of a spirit of despair. They will be called oaks of righteousness, a planting of the LORD for the display of his splendor.
>
> Isaiah 61:1–3

I am believing that what God has for you and for me will come to pass. Only as you live out what He has called *you* to do will we be able to fully experience what He has for *me*.

In a glorious gift from the Lord, heaven comes to earth right where we are in our everyday world. We live out our calling as we pray for a co-worker's healing and as we share the good news of Jesus with a neighbor and as we intercede for our local government decision-makers. Jesus has designed His Body that way: The Body itself works "as each part does its work" (Ephesians 4:16).

You may not believe that you can be part of a "future history" that will bring about a revival and reformation. But I believe in you. And way more important, Jesus believes in you. You were made to be a grace distributor for the high King of heaven.

History has many precedents. One of my favorites happened in New York City in 1857 when a revival broke out after a businessman named Jeremiah Lanphier started a noontime prayer meeting. His church had appointed him as a "city missionary," and not knowing what to do, he prayed a simple prayer: "Lord, what wilt Thou have me to do?" The answer to that prayer led him to start a prayer meeting during business hours that would ultimately result in one million souls being brought to Jesus. Led by a businessman, it was a prayer revival that had a major impact on cities across America, Canada, England, Scotland and Wales.[1]

Four Suggestions for Your Work

What can you do to be part of the grace distributed second Reformation? I have four suggestions for your work in the marketplace. You can also apply these suggestions to your circumstances at school, in church and in your family.

1. Know You Have an Assignment.

You have an assignment in the marketplace. This is a super-important place to start. I hope I have convinced you of this in the previous pages. Your vocation is not a curse; it is a calling. You are on assignment for God. You are a precious son or daughter of His, and He has placed you where there is opportunity. He has a mission for you to accomplish. You are a missionary in the marketplace!

Whatever you do, work at it with all your heart, as working for the Lord, not for human masters, since you know that you will receive an inheritance from the Lord as a reward. It is the Lord Christ you are serving.

Colossians 3:23–24

Ideally, I would love for your church to commission you, like Jeremy Lanphier, as a marketplace missionary and recognize you as a distributor of grace at your address and in your position.

Start by recognizing who you are. Walk through your workplace each morning and evening as a heavenly ambassador, asking the Holy Spirit to use you as His Kingdom representative. I think you will be overwhelmed at His goodness when you see how He uses you every single day.

2. Offer Your Work as Worship.

Offer your work as an act of worship. "Whatever you do, whether in word or deed, do it all in the name of the Lord Jesus, giving thanks to God the Father through him" (Colossians 3:17).

How you do your work matters to your witness. People want to receive love and grace from someone who does his or her work with excellence and enthusiasm. Since you have been placed in your role on assignment, you have the opportunity, as an act of worship, to be great in the role! Your excelling at your work opens doors for worship to the Master and for others to see your worship and respond to the one true God.

Daniel is one of my favorite characters in the Old Testament. This Jewish captive in Babylon made some bold decisions, including refusing to eat the king's food (thus risking his life and the lives of his friends at the early stage of their captivity) and refusing to stop praying to God, in defiance of the king's decree. The Lord rewarded Daniel's faithfulness. But in addition to those parts of his story, Daniel also excelled past any other of the Babylonian advisers (see Daniel 1:19–20). I guarantee there were some things in Babylonian school that were very different from what he had learned in Hebrew school!

Daniel knew he was representing his God in whatever he did and wherever he went. Scripture records that even when his enemies were seeking to destroy him and discredit his life, they could find nothing in his character or job performance upon which to accuse him. The only thing they could find to attack Daniel on was his faith (see Daniel 6:3–5).

May that be true of us! Then we will have more and more stories of God getting glory in the everyday of our workplace as we see work as an act of worship.

3. Reach Out with Love.

Reach out to your co-workers with love and grace. Jesus said, "Let your light shine before others, that they may see your good deeds and glorify your Father in heaven" (Matthew 5:16).

As we have noted, many in our culture expect Christians to be mean, angry, condemning and judgmental. When we come to people in the opposite spirit, we have the opportunity to distribute grace in the power of the Holy Spirit. The truth about followers of Jesus is that we are the singular greatest source of compassion on the planet, the first to scenes of disaster and last to leave in times of crisis. Starting in first-century Rome, it has been the believers in Jesus who rescued babies from trash heaps and cared for those with the plague, while the civic leaders and wealthier classes abandoned the cities.

Historian Rodney Stark studied the first-century pandemics and included one such description of the behavior of believers from Dionysius, bishop of Corinth around the year 171:

> Most of our brother Christians showed unbounded love and loyalty, never sparing themselves and thinking only of one another. Heedless of danger, they took charge of the sick, attending to their every need and ministering to them in Christ, and with them departed this life serenely happy; for they were infected by others with the disease, drawing on themselves the sickness of their neighbors and cheerfully accepting their pains. Many, in nursing and curing others, transferred their death to themselves and died in their stead. . . . The best of our brothers lost their lives in this manner, a number of presbyters, deacons, and laymen winning high commendation so that death in this form, the result of great piety and strong faith, seems in every way the equal of martyrdom.[2]

You can be a prayer warrior, a ministering presence and a manifestation of the love of the Father to those in your cubicle, warehouse or carpool.

4. Witness to Your Co-Workers.

Witness to your co-workers with the good news of God's love.

Paul wrote:

> All this is from God, who reconciled us to himself through Christ and gave us the ministry of reconciliation: that God was reconciling the world to himself in Christ, not counting people's sins against them. And he has committed to us the message of reconciliation. We are therefore

Christ's ambassadors, as though God were making his appeal through us. We implore you on Christ's behalf: Be reconciled to God.

2 Corinthians 5:18–20

Bringing heaven to earth is a proclamation of the Father's love to those outside the household of faith. Sharing the Gospel—the great news that Jesus Christ is God come in the flesh and that He has demonstrated His love for us by dying on the cross for our sins "while we were still sinners" (Romans 5:8)—is our powerful assignment as His followers. We are His ambassadors, literally "begging" our families, friends, co-workers and communities to come to the knowledge of the Savior.

God has placed you strategically in your marketplace setting. You are who you are and where you are as a Kingdom assignment. The Spirit of God has called and equipped you for such a moment as this. The heavenly love of God flows from the Father through the Son and is empowered by the Spirit in your life. You bring heaven to earth and are a distributor of grace on behalf of the King of the universe!

Heaven on earth will bring revival to the world as dark places become full of the light and love of Christ. Heaven on earth makes Jesus the center of it all (see Colossians 1:18) and recognizes you as His ambassador through the power of the Holy Spirit.

Please join me in praying for and participating in the launch of the second Reformation as we see the wonderful, amazing, matchless grace of Jesus manifested on planet earth. Let's start with you and me and experience what the Lord can do with surrendered hearts.

BEFORE YOU GO

Do you believe you are "on assignment" in life? Would your church consider commissioning you as a marketplace ambassador? Do you have people in your life who can pray with you about those you are influencing in your workplace? Is there training you need to help you move to the next level of effectiveness in your Kingdom assignment?

14

THE REST OF THE STORY

James and Rebecca had navigated so many peaks and pits in their life together that it was hard to recount them all. With a teenager, a school-age child and an "almost," their family of nearly five was full and flourishing. Rebecca was teaching in the kids' school and James was now a senior project manager at work. Both had seen miracles of salvation and healing—at work, at school and in the neighborhood—and they felt deeply rooted in the ministry teams of their church family. Most encouraging of all were the foundation and infectious vitality of the faith of their children.

Life had challenges galore, but they walked each day and week in the presence of the Lord. As an amazing bonus gift, both sets of parents were now rooted in thriving churches in their local communities and growing spiritually.

The presence of God on the journey of life made James and Rebecca grateful for His grace and goodness at every turn.

Famous radio personality Paul Harvey used to say, "Now you know . . . the rest of the story." That time has come for us as well. What is the rest of the story for you, for the Church of Jesus Christ and for the Kingdom of God?

Simply put, I believe God will bring about a revival of personal transformation for you. **Your life can and should and must be changed forever as you receive your identity, your calling and your assignment to bring heaven to earth as a distributor of God's grace. Bringing heaven to earth will change your life forever.**

I am also praying for a corporate revival as the Church of Jesus begins to release His grace and goodness to the world in every sphere of culture. The Church will be radiant as the Bride of Christ as we begin to manifest the life and love of Jesus, our Bridegroom, when we gather and when we are distributed. We will be like the father of the Prodigal Son as we run to embrace those who turn to Him. The goodness of God will be made known as we watch Him save, heal and deliver those He calls to Himself.

The Body of Christ will have a "full employment policy" as we are activated to walk in the power of His Spirit. Prayers for salvation and healing will be answered as we see multitudes coming to know Jesus and becoming whole in Him.

The heart of God is redemption. We live and walk, therefore, as redemptive people, always looking to share the life-giving message of our hope in Christ and consistently seeking to walk as Jesus did, full of grace and truth. We manifest the life, love and light of Jesus everywhere we go. We live in a dynamic relationship with the Holy Spirit and bring the salvation, healing and deliverance of Jesus to a dying and broken world. Because of our commitment to Him as the center of gravity in all that we do, we are prepared to live out His announced mission and ministry.

Declaring the Vision

We in the Body of Christ have the creative capacity from the throne of heaven to give birth to new Kingdom realities, including allowing the world to see, sense and experience the goodness of God and be drawn to Him for hope and life (see Matthew 5:13–16).

My friend Ray Johnston, author of *Hope Quotient*, says:

> Nobody ever gets a dream without hope. I know of many leaders around the world, some blessed with great resources and others who have almost nothing, who have made major impacts on their communities. They all have the one thing that nobody can do without—*hope*.[1]

In chapter 12 I mentioned that, over the years in my own faith walk, I have come increasingly to believe and experience what Jesus taught in Matthew 18:19—that there is tremendous power in His children—us!—agreeing on earth.

Since agreement on earth can move heaven, and since the vision of the Church that we have been discussing is from the throne of heaven, I claim it as the will of the Father for this earth. I declare it over our churches and ministries. I pronounce it as a divine mandate over the nations and across the continents of the earth. I say *yes* to the goodness of God. It is His kindness that leads us to repentance (see Romans 2:4), and His people will manifest His kindness to the world around us.

Now is the time to declare the acceptable year of the Lord for salvation and His favor (see 2 Corinthians 6:2). I say we will embrace both the mystery of God's sovereignty and the prayer of faith that it will be "on earth as it is in heaven" (Matthew 6:10).

We know from Scripture that is the will of the Lord that His followers become "oaks of righteousness" (Isaiah 61:3).

Rebuilding, renewing and rejoicing are the inheritance we are to receive as "we live and move and have our being" in Him (Acts 17:28). I am praying for, believing for and living and leading this hour for a victorious Church consecrated to Him, one that lives and loves in such a way that righteousness and praise spring up before all nations.

Join me in a Jesus-centered experience of faith that transforms people, families, churches, communities, states, nations and the world we live in for the glory of God.

The River of Grace

The Kingdom of God will see radical expansion as revival sweeps through the personal lives of men and women and results in cultural transformation. The second Reformation will engender mass transformation across societal structures as we recognize that the enemy of our souls has been deceiving and destroying in the everyday of life. Restoration of relationships, rebuilding of families and homes, reengineering of social values and structures—all will occur in this season of great flourishing.

The calling of the people of God to bring heaven to earth will be manifested in relationships, structures, cultural values and a massive demonstration of hope as we become carriers and distributors of grace and peace in the strong name of Jesus.

And all this will happen because we partner with the Father to bring heaven to earth. We who have received grace become the distributors of grace, and we will watch the most amazing divine ripple effect as the grace of God flows like a river. In fact, the river of grace will overflow through thousands to reach millions, ultimately to reach a billion or more for the glory of His name.

New Testament Christianity was never meant to be for a moment. It is a movement that flows like a river from its heavenly source and brings life to all who receive its healing touch. (See Ezekiel 47:1–12 for one description of that heavenly river.)

And that, my dear reader, is the rest of the story that the Lord of all creation is calling you and me to believe for, to contend for and to distribute on planet earth!

Listen to the testimony of Saul-turned-Paul:

> Mercy kissed me, even though I used to be a blasphemer, a persecutor of believers, and a scorner of what turned out to be true. I was ignorant and didn't know what I was doing. I was flooded with such incredible grace, *like a river overflowing its banks*, until I was full of faith and love for Jesus, the Anointed One!
>
> I can testify that the Word is true and deserves to be received by all, for Jesus Christ came into the world to bring sinners back to life—even me, the worst sinner of all! Yet I was captured by grace, so that Jesus Christ could display through me the outpouring of his Spirit as a pattern to be seen for all those who would believe in him for eternal life.
>
> Because of this my praises rise to the King of all the universe who is indestructible, invisible, and full of glory, the only God who is worthy of the highest honors throughout all of time and throughout the eternity of eternities! Amen!
>
> 1 Timothy 1:13–17 TPT

BEFORE YOU GO

Thank you! Thank you for letting me partner with the Holy Spirit to share what I believe is His clarion call for a second Reformation in our time. Bringing heaven to earth in the everyday distribution of God's love and grace is the gateway for what Jesus has for us in this moment. Revival, renewal and restoration are coming through women and men who have received great grace and have become grace distributors. You are one of them. You have your assignment. It is *Go!* time!

Notes

Chapter 1 How I Became a Grace Ambassador

1. Abraham Joshua Heschel, *Moral Grandeur and Spiritual Audacity: Essays*, ed. Susannah Heschel (New York: Farrar, Straus and Giroux, 1996), viii.

2. You can see a brief video on that subject here, created by the Museum of the Bible in Washington, D.C.: https://www.museumofthebible.org/book-minute/the-gutenberg-press-an-invention-that-changed-the-world.

3. For more on the billion soul harvest, see Breaking Christian News, October 28, 2005, https://www.breakingchristiannews.com/articles/display_art.html?ID=1556.

Chapter 2 Christian Life in the Now

1. Barna Group, March 4, 2015, "What Millennials Want When They Visit Church," https://www.barna.com/research/what-millennials-want-when-they-visit-church/.

2. Ibid.

3. George Barna, "Millennials in America," October 12, 2021, https://www.arizonachristian.edu/wp-content/uploads/2021/10/George-Barna-Millennial-Report-2021-FINAL-Web.pdf.

4. Ibid.

5. Millard Fillmore's Bathtub, https://timpanogos.blog/2009/01/20/quote-of-the-moment-richard-halverson-chaplain-of-the-us-senate/.

6. "Classic and Contemporary Excerpts from August 19, 1991," *Christianity Today*, August 19, 1991, https://www.christianitytoday.com/ct/1991/august-19/reflections-classic-and-contemporary-excerpts.html.

7. Terry M. Crist, *Learning the Language of Babylon—Changing the World by Engaging the Culture* (Grand Rapids: Chosen Books, 2001), 35.

8. Ibid., 101.

9. Dave Hunt, "Christian Activism—Is It Biblical?," September 6, 2021 (originally published November 1, 1989), The Berean Call, https://www .thebereancall.org/content/christian-activism-it-biblical-0.

10. Os Hillman, *Change Agent* (Lake Mary, FL: Charisma House, 2011), xi.

11. For an excellent resource on this subject, see Vishal Mangalwadi, *Truth and Transformaion: A Manifeso for Healing Nations* (Seattle: YWAM Publishing, 2009).

12. Cited in Hillman, 10.

Chapter 4 The Church and the Kingdom

1. Kris Vallotton, Facebook, January 10, 2013, https://www.facebook .com/kvministries/posts/all-of-the-church-is-in-the-kingdom-but-not-all -of-the-kingdom-is-in-the-church-/10151226738853741/.

2. Ed Silvoso, *Ekklesia* (Minneapolis: Chosen, 2017), 36.

3. Ibid., 51, 54.

4. Ibid., 55.

5. For a further study of the contrasts between a Kingdom worldview and a Church worldview, see Joseph Mattera, "Contrasting a Kingdom Mindset with a Church Mindset," December 8, 2016, https://joseph mattera.org/contrasting-a-kingdom-mindset-with-a-church-mindset/.

Chapter 5 The Fivefold Ministry and Spiritual Gifts

1. You may want to read Matthew D. Green's book on the subject, *Understanding the Fivefold Ministry*, with a foreword by Jack Hayford (Lake Mary, Fla.: Charisma House, 2005).

2. I wrote about this in *The Prevailing Church* (Rocklin, Calif.: Jessup University Press, 2020).

3. See here for a brief review with similar thoughts: https://medium .com/koinonia/why-christians-belong-on-a-battleship-and-not-a-cruise -ship-71c2d3834f9f.

4. You can watch Pastor Johnson's articulation of what a Church as an "heircraft carrier" functions like in terms of equipping here: https:// www.thefreedomoutpost.net/15-min-vid-on-carrier-model.

Chapter 8 The Foundation of Spiritual Gifts

1. Arthur T. Pierson, *The Making of a Sermon* (New York: Gospel Publishing House, second edition, 1907), 187.

Chapter 9 Spiritual Gifts for the Second Reformation

1. John Stott, *The Contemporary Christian* (Downers Grove, Ill.: InterVarsity, 1992), 24, 29.

Chapter 10 Grace in the Marketplace

1. Rodney Stark, *The Victory of Reason* (New York: Random House, 2006), xi.
2. For more information on William Jessup University, see www .jessup.edu.
3. Ed Silvoso, *Anointed for Business*, 2nd ed. (2006; repr., Minneapolis: Chosen, 2009), 23.
4. Bob Goff, *Love Does* (Nashville: Thomas Nelson, 2012), 125.

Chapter 11 Sharing Grace with Our World

1. John R. W. Stott, "Authentic Christianity," *Christianity Today*, January 1997, vol. 41, no. 1.
2. Robert Farrar Capon, *Between Noon and Three* (Grand Rapids: Eerdmans, 1997), 165.

Chapter 12 The Spiritual War over Grace

1. Ed Stetzer, *Subversive Kingdom* (Nashville: B & H Books, 2012), 15.
2. Reggie McNeal, *Missional Renaissance* (San Francisco: Jossey-Bass 2009), 45.

Chapter 13 How Faith and Life Intersect for Revival

1. Dan Graves, MSL, "Jeremy Lanphier Led Prayer Revival," Christianity.com, May 3, 2010, https://www.christianity.com/church/church -history/timeline/1801-1900/jeremy-lanphier-led-prayer-revival-11630507 .html.
2. Rodney Stark, *The Rise of Christianity* (Princeton, N.J.: Princeton University Press, 1991), 82.

Chapter 14 The Rest of the Story

1. Ray Johnston, "The Four Things That Only Hope Can Do, Part 3: Hope Sets You Free to Dream," *The Hope Quotient*, May 29, 2014, http://hopequotient.com/blog/four-things-hope-can-part-3-hope-sets -free-dream/#more-111.

Dr. John Jackson is the sixth president of William Jessup University (www.jessup.edu) in Rocklin, California. Since becoming president in 2011, John has led the university to triple in size; to add math, sciences and arts, graduate programs and online programs to its curricular offerings; and to become regionally and nationally ranked by *U.S. News & World Report* and *The Chronicle of Higher Education*. Jessup's goal is for its students to become *equipped and known*.

Dr. Jackson has demonstrated strong communication, strategic and organizational leadership skills in his work with national and global organizations and ministries. He has written or co-authored nine books on leadership and spiritual formation and is a sought-after speaker and consultant.

Prior to joining William Jessup University, John served as the executive director of Thriving Churches International and as a lead pastor of Bayside Church in Granite Bay, California. He was the founding pastor of LifePoint Church in Minden, Nevada, and the executive minister of the American Baptist Churches of the Pacific Southwest (now Transformation Ministries), where he worked with more than 270 churches in four Western states and served on nine corporate boards. John also served as the senior pastor and in several staff roles at First Baptist Church of Oxnard and as the youth pastor at First Baptist Church of Buena Park (both in California).

John earned his Ph.D. and M.A. in educational administration and organizational studies from the University of California, Santa Barbara; his M.A. in theology (Christian formation and discipleship) from Fuller Theological Seminary; and his B.A. in religion (Christian history and thought) from Chapman University.

John is married to Pamela Harrison Jackson. They have five children and four grandchildren and make their home in Northern California.

Other Works by John Jackson

The Prevailing Church

The Right Choice

30 Days to Healthier Relationships

Leveraging Your Communication Style

Leveraging Your Leadership Style

God-Size Your Church

Finding Your Place in God's Plan

Pastorpreneur

High Impact Church Planting

For additional resources, please visit the author's website at www.drjohnjackson.com. You can also find John on Instagram and Facebook (@wjuprez for both).

PERSONAL NOTES